THIS BOOK BELONGS TO

Alice Walters

DATE

Sept. 15, 2009

LISTENING TO GOD SERIES

BY GLEN S. R. CARLSON

Listening - A journey with Jesus day by day
Devotions for each day of the year. *(December 2007)*

Listening 2 - The Father's love
Listening to Jesus in the Book of First John and in the Parable of the Prodigal *(August 2009)*

Listening 3 - Planting Feet
Listening to Jesus through Luther's Small Catechism *(June 2009)*

Listening 4 - Jesus: Priest and King
Listening to Jesus through the Book of Hebrews *(December 2009)*

PLANTING FEET

Planting feet firmly in Jesus' Kingdom is an absolute. Planting begins at birth and continues throughout life. "Planting Feet" is a tool that uses the foundation principles as you begin your walk with Jesus. "Planting Feet" is part of the Listenting to God Series which gives a personal message from Jesus for you each day

Listening3

Planting Feet

Confirming My Faith
Day by Day

by Glen S.R. Carlson

Listening3 Planting Feet, Confirming My Faith Day by Day

Published by:
Listening to God Ministries
Glen S.R. Carlson
Box 2572
Stony Plain, AB Canada
T7Z 1X9
listeningtogod@canadasurfs.ca

Also by Glen,
Listening: A Journey with Jesus Day by Day, 2007

ISBN 978-1-897544-10-5

DIGITALLY PRINTED IN CANDA BY

Dedicated to
My grandchildren
who have confirmed their faith
in Jesus Christ
through Confirmation
in the Lutheran Church.
Selim, Stefan, Anders
Aline, Elsa (to be soon)

CONTENTS

SUGGESTED LESSON PLAN

INTRODUCTION

The concept of Confirmation in the Churches is very good. It certainly follows the instruction of Jesus to teach and make disciples. It also follows the admonition of Martin Luther who developed the Small Catechism as a tool to teach and instruct people of all ages in the Christian Faith. However pastors and teachers in the churches where the nuts and bolts of confirmation take place have often been frustrated as to how to teach confirmation so it has a lasting quality. In many churches confirmation has become a graduation process. Young people are leaving the church rather than becoming involved in Kingdom ministry. Martin Luther's understanding was that confirmation was to take place in the home where parents actually do the teaching rather than sending their youth to the church to be taught by the pastor or assigned teacher. Many ideas and combination of ideas have been tried but we still find our youth graduate What to do.

Following is another concept. This can be used at any age or grade. It is based on three principles.

1. **Listening each day.** The emphasis is to learn to listen to Jesus whether using the Bible or using the Catechism. God has a message for each person each day of the week. What is that message?

2. **Journal each day.** For some this may be difficult. Journaling does not have to be much. It could be one or two words or a whole series of thoughts and ideas that one feels Jesus is saying to you. The reading time could take place as an individual or as a family.

3. **Discussion.** Take a moment in class to discuss the topics for that week. Good discussion questions to ask as you come to the word at the end of each lesson are the five "W's" WHO, WHAT, WHEN, WHERE and WHY.

CONFIRMATION IS

Confirmation, **what is it**
But a journey in life
With Jesus at your side
To lead the Way.

Luke 24:15 Suddenly, Jesus himself came along and joined them and began walking beside them.

Confirmation is **preparing**
For the journey ahead
As you make the decisions
That leads to life.

John 10:10 The thief's purpose is to steal and kill and destroy. My purpose is to give life in all its fullness.

Confirmation is **birthing**
From the beginning of life
Eager to listen
To the Word from above.

Jeremiah 1:5 "I knew you before I formed you in your mother's womb. Before you were born I set you apart and appointed you as my spokesman to the world."

Confirmation is **commitment**
To Jesus who teaches
The lessons of life
As you grow in the faith.

John 13:8 - 9 "No," Peter protested, "you will never wash my feet!" Jesus replied, "But if I don't wash you, you won't belong to me." 9Simon Peter exclaimed, "Then wash my hands and head as well, Lord, not just my feet!"

Confirmation is **affirming**
The covenant of Baptism
Becoming part of the Kingdom
Through Water and the Word.

John 3:5 Jesus replied, "The truth is, no one can enter the Kingdom of God without being born of water and the Spirit.

Confirmation makes a **statement**
Of what you believe
About Jesus as Lord
And Saviour of your life.

John 11:25 Jesus told her, "I am the resurrection and the life. Those who believe in me, even though they die like everyone else, will live again.

Confirmation is **confessing**
The words of the Creed
So become aware
Of what you believe.

John 3:16 "For God so loved the world that he gave his only Son, so that everyone who believes in him will not perish but have eternal life.

Confirmation is **admitting**
The Need for a Saviour
For the sins in your life
And the sins of the world.

Romans 3:23 For all have sinned; all fall short of God's glorious standard.

Confirmation is **prayer**
As you talk to Jesus
When He listens as promised
To our concerns in life.

Matthew 26:41 Keep alert and pray. Otherwise temptation will overpower you. For though the spirit is willing enough, the body is weak!"

Confirmation is **responsibility**
In the Kingdom called Church
Taking on the tasks
Using God-given gifts.

1 Corinthians 12:4 Now there are different kinds of spiritual gifts, but it is the same Holy Spirit who is the source of them all.

Confirmation is **relationship**
In the Kingdom of God
As you work with God's people
To carry out His plan.

Acts 6:7 God's message was preached in ever-widening circles. The number of believers greatly increased in Jerusalem, and many of the Jewish priests were converted, too.

Confirmation is **anointing**
From the Father above
With the oil of blessing
As the commission to life.

1 Samuel 16:13 So as David stood there among his brothers, Samuel took the olive oil he had brought and poured it on David's head. And the Spirit of the LORD came mightily upon him from that day on.

Confirmation is **continuous**
From beginning to end
As you confirm your faith
Every day of your life.

Deuteronomy 17:19 He must always keep this copy of the law with him and read it daily as long as he lives. That way he will learn to fear the LORD his God by obeying all the terms of this law.

Confirmation is **feasting**
In the supper of Jesus
To have fellowship with Him
And the Body of Christ.

Matthew 26:26 - 28 As they were eating, Jesus took a loaf of bread and asked God's blessing on it. Then he broke it in pieces and gave it to the disciples, saying, "Take it and eat it, for this is my body." 27And he took a cup of wine and gave thanks to God for it. He gave it to them and said, "Each of you drink from it, 28for this is my blood, which seals the covenant between God and his people. It is poured out to forgive the sins of many.

Confirmation is **death**
Accepting Jesus on the Cross
Which leads you to life
In the Resurrection of Christ.

2 Corinthians 5:15 He died for everyone so that those who receive his new life will no longer live to please themselves. Instead, they will live to please Christ, who died and was raised for them.

Confirmation is **influence**
As you go into the world
Telling people of Jesus
To accept Him as Lord.

Acts 1:8 But when the Holy Spirit has come upon you, you will receive power and will tell people about me everywhere—in Jerusalem, throughout Judea, in Samaria, and to the ends of the earth."

Confirmation is **fulfillment**
Of the Promise of God
That He will be with you
As Long as you live.

Matthew 28:20 Teach these new disciples to obey all the commands I have given you. And be sure of this: I am with you always, even to the end of the age."

THE TEN COMMANDMENTS

Exodus 20:1 - 17 [1]Then God instructed the people as follows:
[2]"I am the LORD your God, who rescued you from slavery in
Egypt. [3]"**Do not worship any other gods besides me.** [4]"Do
not make idols of any kind, whether in the shape of birds or
animals or fish. [5]You must never worship or bow down to
them, for I, the LORD your God, am a jealous God who will
not share your affection with any other god! I do not leave
unpunished the sins of those who hate me, but I punish the
children for the sins of their parents to the third and fourth
generations. [6]But I lavish my love on those who love me and
obey my commands, even for a thousand generations. [7]"**Do
not misuse the name of the LORD your God.** The LORD
will not let you go unpunished if you misuse his name.

[8]"**Remember to observe the Sabbath day by keeping it holy.**
[9]Six days a week are set apart for your daily duties and regular
work, [10]but the seventh day is a day of rest dedicated to the
LORD your God. On that day no one in your household
may do any kind of work. This includes you, your sons and
daughters, your male and female servants, your livestock, and
any foreigners living among you. [11]For in six days the LORD
made the heavens, the earth, the sea and everything in them;
then he rested on the seventh day. That is why the LORD
blessed the Sabbath day and set it apart as holy.

[12]"**Honor your father and mother.** Then you will live a long,
full life in the land the LORD your God will give you. [13]"**Do
not murder.** [14]"**Do not commit adultery.** [15]"**Do not steal.**
[16]"**Do not testify falsely against your neighbor.** [17]"**Do not
covet your neighbor's house. Do not covet your neighbor's
wife,** male or female servant, ox or donkey, or anything else
your neighbor owns."

Check on the internet
YouTube – Ten Commandments.

THE TEN COMMANDMENTS

The First Commandment

You shall have no other gods.

What does this mean?

We should fear, love and trust in God above all things.

The Second Commandment

You shall not misuse the name of the Lord your God.

What does this mean?

We should fear and love God so that we do not curse, swear, use satanic arts, lie, or deceive by His name, but call upon it in every trouble, pray, praise, and give thanks.

The Third Commandment

Remember the Sabbath day by keeping it holy.

What does this mean?

We should fear and love God so that we do not despise preaching and His Word, but hold it sacred and gladly hear and learn it.

The Fourth Commandment

Honor your father and your mother.

What does this mean?

We should fear and love God so that we do not despise or anger our parents and other authorities, but honor them, serve and obey them, love and cherish them.

The Fifth Commandment

You shall not murder.

What does this mean?

We should fear and love God so that we do not hurt or harm our neighbor in his body, but help and support him in every physical need.

The Sixth Commandment

You shall not commit adultery.

What does this mean?

We should fear and love God so that we lead a sexually pure and decent life in what we say and do, and husband and wife love and honor each other.

The Seventh Commandment

You shall not steal.

What does this mean?

We should fear and love God so that we do not take our neighbor's money or possessions, or get them in any dishonest way, but help him to improve and protect his possessions and income.

The Eighth Commandment

You shall not give false testimony against your neighbor.

What does this mean?

We should fear and love God so that we do not tell lies about our neighbor, betray him, slander him, or hurt his reputation, but defend him, speak well of him, and explain everything in the kindest possible way.

The Ninth Commandment

You shall not covet your neighbor's house.

What does this mean?

We should fear and love God so that we do not scheme to get our neighbor's inheritance or house, or get it in a way which only appears right, but help and be of service to him in keeping it.

The Tenth Commandment

You shall not covet your neighbor's wife, or his manservant, or maidservant, his ox or donkey, or anything that belongs to your neighbor.

What does this mean?

We should fear and love God so that we do not entice or force away our neighbor's wife, workers, or animals, or turn them against him, but urge them to stay and do their duty.

The Close of the Commandments

What does God say about all of these commandments?

He says, "I, the Lord your God, am a jealous God, punishing the children for the sin of the fathers to the third and fourth generation of those who hate Me, but showing love to a thousand generations of those who love Me and keep My commandments" (Exodus 20:5-6).

What does this mean?

God threatens to punish all who break these commandments. Therefore, we should fear His wrath and not do anything against them. But He promises grace and every blessing to all who keep these commandments. Therefore, we should also love and trust in Him and gladly do what He commands.

Day 1

FIRST COMMANDMENT

I am the Lord your God.
You shall have no other gods.

Exodus 20: [3]"Do not worship any other gods besides me.
[4]"Do not make idols of any kind, whether in the shape of
birds or animals or fish."

JESUS SPEAKS OF FEAR

This is the first and most important
  of all the commandments.
By obeying this commandment
  I come first in your life.
This commandment becomes the foundation
  for all the other commandments.
To obey this commandment you must
  Fear Me, Love Me, Trust Me.
Loving Me
  is the foundation of loving yourself.
Loving Me is centered on fear.
Fearing Me
  is not being afraid of Me
  but it is being respectful toward Me.
It is out of respect
  that you will put Me first in your life
  that you will listen to Me
  that you will obey Me.
My love is expressed in justice.
  By fearing Me you accept My justice.
In this way you become a part of Me,
  and I become a part of you.

MY RESPONSE

Write in your journal and/or share in your facebook/ blog what the word "Fear" means to you.

Day 2

FIRST COMMANDMENT

I am the Lord your God.
You shall have no other gods.

JESUS SPEAKS OF LOVE

Loving Me
is centered on My love.
It is because of this love
that I created you in My image.
Being created in My image
I have given you a special gift
which is to be treasured and protected.
It is the gift of choice.
This gift of choice has the ability to
expand the mind to new horizons
accept or reject Me as your partner in life
decide to live a good life or an evil life.
The gift of My image
makes you free to love Me.
My love is expressed in truth;
Your desire for truth
is an expression of My love.

MY RESPONSE

Write in your journal and/or share in your facebook/ blog word "Love" means to you.

Day 3

FIRST COMMANDMENT

I am the Lord your God.
You shall have no other gods.

JESUS SPEAKS OF TRUST

Trusting Me
is centered on faith.
Trust, mercy and faith work hand in hand.
Trust is an expression of My love
When you trust Me you also love Me.
Mercy is also an expression of My love
When you love me you are merciful.
When you have faith in Me
I give you the ability to trust yourself
I make it possible for you to be at peace
I give you a greater ability to risk.
Putting faith in me
is not a weakness as some think
but a strength that is needed.
Faith in Me:
sets you free from worry
strengthens our relationship
allows Me to have faith in You.
In our relationship
it is necessary for you to
Fear, Love, and Trust Me
above everything.

MY RESPONSE

Write in your journal and/or share in your facebook/ blog what the word "Trust" means to you.

Day 4

SECOND COMMANDMENT

You shall not take the name of the Lord your God in vain.

Exodus 20 [7]"Do not misuse the name of the LORD your God. The LORD will not let you go unpunished if you misuse his name.

JESUS SPEAKS ABOUT HIS NAME

Because you fear and love Me
you will keep this commandment
by honoring My Name.
The reason you honor My Name
is because I am holy
and your obedience makes you holy.
Holiness comes from Me
so you are holy only in My presence.
When you misuse My Name
you are no longer holy.
When you use My Name superstitiously
you become clouded with witchcraft.
When you use My Name to curse or swear
you are dabbling in evil thoughts.
When you use My Name deceitfully
you are breaking our relationship.
It is in My Name
that every knee shall bow and
every tongue confess that I am Lord.

MY RESPONSE

Write in your journal and/or share in your facebook/ blog what the word "holy" means to you.

Day 5

SECOND COMMANDMENT

You shall not take the name of the Lord your God in vain.

JESUS SPEAKS OF HIS NAME

My Name
   must be at the center of all your **prayer.**
For when you pray in My Name
   you are calling on Me
   I will hear you
   I will intercede before the Father and
   I will answer you.
My Name
   must be at the center of all your **praise.**
When you praise in My Name:
   you are worshipping Me
   you acknowledge all that I have done
   you are giving Me the Glory.
My Name
   must be at the center of all your **thanksgiving.**
For when you give thanks in My Name:
   you recognize that all things come from Me
   you are receiving a blessing from Me
   you are sharing the abundance with others.

MY RESPONSE

Write in your journal and/or share in your facebook/ blog what the word "Name" means to you.

Day 6

THE THIRD COMMANDMENT

Remember the Sabbath day to keep it holy.

Exodus 20 [8]"Remember to observe the Sabbath day by keeping it holy. [9]Six days a week are set apart for your daily duties and regular work, [10]but the seventh day is a day of rest dedicated to the LORD your God."

JESUS SPEAKS ABOUT THE SABBATH

The first commandment recognizes Me.
The Second Commandment honors Me.
The Third Commandment
establishes a relationship with Me.
When you REMEMBER THE SABBATH DAY
you become aware of My presence
every moment of every day.
Remembering the Sabbath Day
is recognizing the Sabbath Day every day
and not just one day a week.
Remembering the Sabbath Day
is putting praise on your lips 24-7 of every week.
Remembering the Sabbath Day
is making the Sabbath a life style
by living all that I teach you.
Remembering the Sabbath Day
is putting Me in the driver's seat of your life.
We journey together
to see the world My Father created.

MY RESPONSE

Write in your journal and/or share in your facebook/ blog what the word "Sabbath" means to you.

Day 7

THE THIRD COMMANDMENT

Remember the Sabbath day to keep it holy.

JESUS SPEAKS ABOUT HOLINESS

Remembering the Sabbath Day
  is recognizing that holiness
  is an action of My presence
  and not an action of your doing.
Remembering the Sabbath Day
  is developing a hunger for My written word
  and gladly hearing and learning it.
Remembering the Sabbath Day
  is entering into a concert of prayer
  for prayer is the gift of relationship.
Remembering the Sabbath Day
  is developing a habit of worship
  joining My body of believers
  giving praise to My Holy Name.
Remembering the Sabbath Day
  is keeping the laws of My Kingdom
  so you can live in harmony with one another.

MY RESPONSE

Write in your journal and/or share in your facebook/ blog what the word "Sunday" means to you.

Day 8

THE THIRD COMMANDMENT

Remember the Sabbath day to keep it holy.

JESUS SPEAKS ABOUT REST

Remembering the Sabbath Day
  is understanding the need for rest
  just as My Father in creation rested.
Remembering the Sabbath Day
  is taking your faith
  into the marketplace
  of your home and of your work.
Remembering the Sabbath Day
  is putting Me into the midst
  of all that you do.
Remembering the Sabbath Day
  is not worshipping one day
  but worshipping every day
  from morning to night.
Remembering the Sabbath Day
  is going to bed at night
  resting in My presence
  and knowing that I am watching over you.

MY RESPONSE

Write in your journal and/or share in your facebook/ blog what the word "Rest" means to you.

Day 9

FOURTH COMMANDMENT

Honor your father and mother.

Exodus 20 [12]"Honor your father and mother. Then you will live a long, full life in the land the LORD your God will give you.

JESUS SPEAKS OF HONOR

The Key word in this commandment
  is **honor.**
To obey this commandment
  you first must honor Me.
To **honor**
  is a continuous discovery
  for honor comes from Me.
In honor you will discover that:
  Respect moves Me to your level,
  as I bless you into the level of others.
  Obey moves Me into your space
  as I bless you into the space of others.
  Love moves Me to your care
  as I bless you to care for others.
  Serve moves Me as your servant
  as I bless you into Servanthood.
  Esteem moves Me to admire you
  as I bless you to admire others.

MY RESPONSE

Write in your journal and/or share in your facebook/ blog what the word "Honor" means to you.

Day 10

FOURTH COMMANDMENT

Honor your father and mother.

JESUS SPEAKS OF RELATIONSHIPS

To **Dishonor**
comes from the enemy
who desires to destroy relationships.
Dishonor leads you to:
Despise placing a curse
at the expense of a blessing.
Provoke creates dissension
at the expense of peace.
For you to honor your **parents**
moves you to
respect, obey, love, serve and esteem them.
For you to dishonor your parents
moves you to
despise and provoke them.
For you to honor your **children**
moves you to
respect, obey, love, serve and esteem them.
For you to dishonor your children
moves you to
despise and provoke them.

MY RESPONSE

Write in your journal and/or share in your facebook/ blog what the word "Dishonor" means to you.

Day 11

FOURTH COMMANDMENT

Honor your father and mother.

JESUS SPEAKS OF BATTLEFIELDS

There will be times when honor will **be difficult**
for you are on a battle field.
The enemy will work on areas of weakness
to destroy relationships.
He will see that:
you are too busy to build relationships,
you are too angry at the ones you love,
you are too negative to understand others,
you are too selfish to share,
you are too controlling to help,
you are too depressed to love,
you are too anxious to be at peace.
When you **honor as I honor**
it is a joy to make others happy,
it is a joy to be helpful,
it is a joy to be generous,
it is a joy to be a volunteer,
it is a joy to be a servant,
it is a joy to raise others up.

MY RESPONSE

Write in your journal and/or share in your facebook/ blog what the word "Battlefield" means to you.

Day 12

FOURTH COMMANDMENT

Honor your father and mother.

JESUS SPEAKS OF PRIORITIES

To **honor**
  means that you **set priorities.**
Because God is the creator and giver of life
  honor of **God** comes first.
Because God has established the family
  to honor your **family** comes second.
Because God has provided work and service
  to honor those in **authority** comes third.
To **honor**
  means that you **practise forgiveness.**
  Letting go of the old wounds
  brings honor to yourself and others.

MY RESPONSE

Write in your journal and/or share in your facebook/ blog what the word "Family" means to you.

Day 13

FOURTH COMMANDMENT

Honor your father and mother.

JESUS SPEAKS OF PROMISE

The **promise** I give when you honor
is that you will live long in the land I give you.
How you keep this commandment
will affect how you live
for the rest of your life.
When you break this commandment
you will live in destructive relationships
for the rest of your life.
This leads to a **death experience.**
When you keep this commandment
you will live in positive relationships
for the rest of your life.
This leads to a **life experience.**
When you follow the Holy Spirit
He will give you the power and the desire
to honor.

MY RESPONSE

Write in your journal and/or share in your facebook/blog what the word "Promise" means to you.

Day 14

FIFTH COMMANDMENT

You shall not kill.

Exodus 20 [13]"Do not murder.

JESUS SPEAKS OF YOUR LIFE

This commandment that My Father has given
shows the value of life.
At the time of creation
My Father created you in Our Image.
For this reason life is sacred
and must not be destroyed.
You honor life
when you believe in Me.
You kill life
when you reject Me.
You honor life
when you promote health.
You kill life
when you neglect the body.

MY RESPONSE

Write in your journal and/or share in your facebook/ blog what the word "Killing" means to you.

Day 15

FIFTH COMMANDMENT

You shall not kill.

JESUS SPEAKS OF ANOTHER'S LIFE

You honor life
  when you help one another.
You kill life
  when you attack one another.
You honor life
  when you correct one another.
You kill life
  when you neglect correction.
You honor life
  when you encourage one another.
You kill life
  when you condemn each other.
You honor life
  when you share with one another.
You kill life
  when you live for yourself.

MY RESPONSE

Write in your journal and/or share in your facebook/ blog what the word "Life" means to you.

Day 16

FIFTH COMMANDMENT

You shall not kill.

JESUS SPEAKS OF SACRED LIFE

The life that My Father has given you
is holy and sacred.
Therefore you must:
love your enemy,
do good to those who hate you,
bless them that curse you,
pray for those who despitefully use you,
treat people how you want to be treated.
Because Life is sacred you should not:
take another person's life,
war with another for selfish gain,
neglect those who are in need,
destroy someone's freedom,
take your own life.

MY RESPONSE

Write in your journal and/or share in your facebook/ blog what the word "Sacred" means to you.

Day 17

SIXTH COMMANDMENT

You shall not commit adultery.

Exodus 20 [14]"Do not commit adultery.

JESUS SPEAKS OF LOVE

When My Father gave this command
We were looking at the very heart
of all relationships, which is 'Love.'
Because love is the heart
the enemy will use love and sexual relationships
in ways that will pervert and turn them to lust.
I forbid such perversion of love because it leads to:
acceptance of infidelity,
acceptance of divorce,
acceptance of homosexuality,
acceptance of common law living,
acceptance of prostitution,
acceptance of child molestation,
acceptance of abuse,
acceptance of pornography,
acceptance of incest,
acceptance of obscenity.

MY RESPONSE

Write in your journal and/or share in your facebook/ blog what the word "Adultery" means to you.

Day 18

SIXTH COMMANDMENT

You shall not commit adultery.

JESUS SPEAKS OF SEX

Sexual relations is a sacred act
when two people become one in marriage.
Sexuality and obligation are
intimately connected and commanded.
Remember in marriage
a partner is set aside for a godly purpose.
Remember in marriage
when you love someone you will not behave in
ways that will bring pain, fear, doubt or insecurity
into one's life, mind or heart.
Remember in marriage
your greatest joy will be to bring happiness to
your spouse for this brings Me joy.
Remember in marriage
there must not be any hint of sexual immorality
or any kind of impurity, or greed because this is sin
and improper for My people.
Remember in marriage
if you commit adultery it is a sin against Me.

MY RESPONSE

Write in your journal and/or share in your facebook/ blog what the word "Sex" means to you.

Day 19

SIXTH COMMANDMENT

You shall not commit adultery.

JESUS SPEAKS OF MARRIAGE

Remember in marriage
you create a home atmosphere that is safe, therefore it is a place you and I love to be.
Remember in marriage
your body is a temple of My Spirit
so honor Me with your body.
Remember in marriage
it is not good to be alone,
therefore you need to spend time together with each other and with Me.
Remember in marriage
your body does not belong to you alone but it also belongs to your spouse.
Remember in marriage
you must submit to each other as you would submit to Me.
Remember in marriage
you must be kind and compassionate to each other just as I am to you.
Remember in marriage
you must love each other just as I have loved the church by giving up My life.

MY RESPONSE

Write in your journal and/or share in your facebook/ blog what the word "Marriage" means to you.

Day 20

SIXTH COMMANDMENT

You shall not commit adultery.

JESUS SPEAKS OF ACCOUNTABILITY

Remember in marriage
you are responsible to your spouse and family
but you are accountable to Me.
Remember in marriage
when you make a vow to love
and be faithful to each other
you do this in My presence.
Remember in marriage
it is not a place to curse each other
but a place to bless each other
and a place to receive My blessing.
Remember in marriage
it is a place where the fruit of My Spirit flourish.
love, joy, peace,
patience, kindness, goodness,
faithfulness, gentleness
and self-control.

MY RESPONSE

Write in your journal and/or share in your facebook/ blog what the word "Vow" means to you.

Day 21

SEVENTH COMMANDMENT

You shall not steal.

Exodus 20 [15]"Do not steal.."

JESUS SPEAKS OF GIFTS

I give this commandment not to steal
to help you remember
that all that you have is a gift from Me.
What you value in your heart
will determine how you respond
to what you possess.
If in your heart you are content
with the treasures you have
you will have no desire to steal.
If your heart's desire
is to want more and more
then you will steal from others.

MY RESPONSE

Write in your journal and/or share in your facebook/ blog what the word "Steal" means to you.

Day 22

SEVENTH COMMANDMENT

You shall not steal.

JESUS SPEAKS OF SKILLS

Take pride in the skills I have given to you
for this will add value
to the gifts you possess.
Take care of your body
and see how you have been blessed
as you share your life skills
with your family and friends.
Take care of your Soul
for this is what makes you unique
as you share your emotions
and renew your mind.
Take care of your spirit
for this draws you to Me
as we walk on life's journey
and grow in our love.

MY RESPONSE

Write in your journal and/or share in your facebook/ blog what the word "Skill" means to you.

Day 23

SEVENTH COMMANDMENT

You shall not steal.

JESUS SPEAKS OF HELPING

The focus of this commandment
is to reach out and help others
rather than take advantage of others
and hurt them instead.
The gift contained in this commandment
is the gift of encouragement
which leads you to help others
rather than take what they have.
In this command you place value
in your neighbors' money and property
and help them to improve
and protect what they have.
When you see someone who needs help
stop and help that person
and don't expect anything in return;
later on you may be the one needing help.

MY RESPONSE

Write in your journal and/or share in your facebook/ blog what the word "Helping" means to you.

Day 24

SEVENTH COMMANDMENT

You shall not steal.

JESUS SPEAKS OF SATISFACTION

When you resist the temptation to steal
you will find that it will strengthen your faith.
It will also give you joy
in the victory you have won.
When you are generous and share with others
it shows you are satisfied with what you have
and it gives you a contentment
that sets you free.
When you make Me the center of your life
you will have no desire to steal from others;
your focus on life is to learn from Me
and share that wealth with all you meet.

MY RESPONSE

Write in your journal and/or share in your facebook/ blog what the word "Satisfy" means to you.

Day 25

EIGHTH COMMANDMENT

You shall not bear false witness against your neighbour.

Exodus 20 [16]"Do not testify falsely against your neighbour."

JESUS SPEAKS OF LYING

My Father and I gave you this command
'You Shall Not Bear False Witness,'
To help you
develop a life of honesty,
develop a good reputation,
develop a life of integrity.
When you lie you join forces with the devil
who is the father of lies.
When you lie you are rejecting My truth
and therefore you cannot know the truth.
When you lie occasionally
you will feel a sense of guilt.
When you lie habitually you lose your awareness
and you have no guilt.
When you lie you seek to protect yourself
rather than seek My protection.
When you lie it kills you spiritually
for it diminishes My Divine glow in you.
When you lie you betray yourself
but you also betray Me.
When you lie you slander yourself
but you also slander Me.
When you lie you smear a person's name
and so you smear My name.
When you lie you insult a person
and so you insult Me.

MY RESPONSE

Write in your journal and/or share in your facebook/ blog what the word "Lying" means to you.

Day 26

EIGHTH COMMANDMENT

You shall not bear false witness against your neighbour.

JESUS SPEAKS OF TELLING THE TRUTH

When you tell the truth
  you can then believe in yourself.
When you tell the truth
  you begin to understand My truth.
When you tell the truth
  people will trust you in all things.
When you tell the truth
  people will speak well of you
  because they can believe in you.
When you tell the truth
  you destroy Satan's hold on you.
When you tell the truth
  kindness and goodness are a part of you.
When you tell the truth
  you are set free.

MY RESPONSE

Write in your journal and/or share in your facebook/ blog what the word "Truth" means to you.

Day 27

THE NINTH AND TENTH COMMANDMENTS

You shall not covet your neighbor's house.
You shall not covet your neighbor's manservant or his maidservant or his cattle or anything that is your neighbour's.

Exodus 20 [17]"Do not covet your neighbor's house. Do not covet your neighbor's wife, male or female servant, ox or donkey, or anything else your neighbor owns."

JESUS SPEAKS OF COVETING

I say do not covet for coveting is sin.
It gives you a desire to destroy what you have.
   I say do not covet because then you come first
   In all formed relationship, looking out for you.
I say do not covet for coveting makes you jealous
And then you cannot praise what others have done.
   I say do not covet what others possess,
   Whether house or big car for it corrupts your heart.
I say do not covet when others have great love
For your tendency will be to run in the end.
   I say do not covet by desiring what others might have
   For you cannot help others to keep what they have.
I say do not covet, by coaxing another's friend
And make them your friend, by dishonoring all others
   I say do not covet and desire great possessions,
   For you will soon learn they never satisfy.

MY RESPONSE

Write in your journal and/or share in your facebook/blog what the word "Covet" means to you.

Day 28

THE NINTH AND TENTH COMMANDMENTS

JESUS SPEAKS OF COVETING

I say do not covet but rather instead
You should always improve yourself and your friends.
  I say do not covet, but rather reach out
  To share the great love you received as My blessing.
I say do not covet for it leads to greed
And other vices of gambling and stealing.
  I say do not covet by cheating and untruth
  Then you take advantage, thinking you can be
  blessed.
I say do not covet for then you plot and scheme
With thoughts of doing wrong, blemishing your friends.
  I say do not covet leading to false witness
  It makes you look good under false pretenses.
I say do not covet for it dirties the mind
What you need is a renewed mind instead.
  I say do not covet for it destroys your heart
  And it leads to the breaking of My heart as well.

MY RESPONSE

Write in your journal and/or share in your facebook/ blog what the word "Greed" means to you.

Day 29

THE NINTH AND TENTH COMMANDMENTS

JESUS SAYS WHAT TO COVET

Covet can mean to delight in, with joy
And help others rejoice in the things they possess.
What you should covet is to desire My gifts
To grow in your wisdom and your love in Me.
What you should covet is when morals are high
Outweighing material possessions, giving a good life.
What you should covet is when you help others
You covet for good to improve what they have.
A person is wealthy when at peace
Being content with the possessions they already have.
A person is wealthy when they put Me first
They honor My Name and covet My blessing.
So coveting is good when you respect each other
And desire to be in the House of the Lord.
So always be satisfied with the things you have
Giving thanks to your Father who has given you life.

MY RESPONSE

Write in your journal and/or share in your facebook/ blog what the word "Desire" means to you.

The Apostle'sCreed

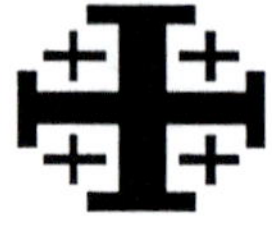

LUTHER'S SMALL CATECHISM

The First Article: Creation
I believe in God, the Father Almighty, Maker of heaven and earth.

What does this mean?

I believe that God has made me and all creatures; that He has given me my body and soul, eyes, ears, and all my members, my reason and all my senses, and still takes care of them. He also gives me clothing and shoes, food and drink, house and home, wife and children, land, animals, and all I have. He richly and daily provides me with all that I need to support this body and life. He defends me against all danger and guards and protects me from all evil. All this He does only out of fatherly, divine goodness and mercy, without any merit or worthiness in me. For all this it is my duty to thank and praise, serve and obey Him. This is most certainly true.

The Second Article: Redemption
And in Jesus Christ, His only Son, our Lord, who was conceived by the Holy Spirit, born of the Virgin Mary, suffered under Pontius Pilate, was crucified, died and was buried. He descended into hell. The third day He rose again from the dead. He ascended into heaven and sits at the right hand of God, the Father Almighty. From thence He will come to judge the living and the dead.

What does this mean?

I believe that Jesus Christ, true God, begotten of the Father from eternity, and also true man, born of the Virgin Mary, is my Lord. Who has redeemed me, a lost and condemned person, purchased and won me from all sins, from death, and from the power of the devil; not with gold or silver, but with His holy, precious blood and with His innocent suffering and death, that I may be His own and live under Him in His kingdom and serve Him in everlasting righteousness, innocence, and blessedness, just as He is risen from the dead, lives and reigns to all eternity. This is most certainly true.

The Third Article: Sanctification

I believe in the Holy Spirit, the holy Christian church, the communion of saints, the forgiveness of sins, the resurrection of the body, and the life everlasting. Amen.

What does this mean?

I believe that I cannot by my own reason or strength believe in Jesus Christ, my Lord, or come to Him; but the Holy Spirit has called me by the Gospel, enlightened me with His gifts, sanctified and kept me in the true faith. In the same way He calls, gathers, enlightens, and sanctifies the whole Christian church on earth, and keeps it with Jesus Christ in the one true faith. In this Christian church He daily and richly forgives all my sins and the sins of all believers. On the Last Day He will raise me and all the dead, and give eternal life to me and all believers in Christ. This is most certainly true.

Check on the Internet
You tube – Apostle's Creed

Day 30

THE FIRST ARTICLE

I BELIEVE IN GOD THE FATHER ALMIGHTY CREATOR OF HEAVEN AND EARTH

JESUS SPEAKS TO ME OF FATHER

When you believe in My Father
it captivates your mind.
When your believe in My Father
you put your total trust in Him
even in times of darkness.
When you believe in My Father
you put your life in his hands
because He cares for you and loves you.
When you believe in My Father
you give your love to Him
as I give My love to you.
When you believe in My Father
it establishes a relationship
between the Divine and the Human
When you believe in My Father.

MY RESPONSE

Write in your journal and/or share on your facebook/ blog what the word "Father" means to you.

Day 31

I BELIEVE IN GOD THE FATHER ALMIGHTY CREATOR OF HEAVEN AND EARTH

JESUS SPEAKS TO ME OF "GOD"

Today think of God.

As God, I am All powerful.
As God, I am present everywhere.
As God, I am all knowing.
As God, I created the world,
 in which you can live your life.
As God, I created the sun, moon and stars,
 to guide you through life.
As God, I created the land, water, and vegetation,
 to give you a home in which to live.
As God, I created the animals, fish, and birds,
 to give you food to eat.
As God, I created the seasons,
 to show my faithfulness.
As God, I created Man
 to have dominion over the earth.
As God, I created Woman
 to be fruitful and multiply.
As God, I created you in My Image
 so we could be family.
As God, I gave you freedom
 to learn to trust Me.
As God, I gave you My Son,
 to show you My love.
As God, I AM.

MY RESPONSE

Write in your journal and/or share on your facebook/ blog what the word "God" means to you.

Day 32

I BELIEVE IN GOD THE FATHER ALMIGHTY CREATOR OF HEAVEN AND EARTH

JESUS SPEAKS TO ME OF "FATHER"

As Father I reach out to you
  in the hand of love
As Father I care for you
  when you are hurting
As Father I love you
  and want to show you My father's love
As Father I will teach you
  the ways of life
As Father I will discipline you
  when you choose wrong
As Father I will forgive you
  when you ask for forgiveness
As Father I will be with you
  all the times
As Father I will pray for you
  in all circumstances
As Father I will give you
  the gifts needed to live
As Father I provide food and drink
  for the table
As Father I will covet
  our relationship.

MY RESPONSE

Write in your journal and/or share in your facebook/ blog what the word "God" means to you.

Day 33

I BELIEVE IN GOD THE FATHER ALMIGHTY CREATOR OF HEAVEN AND EARTH

JESUS SPEAKS OF CREATION

At creation
The Father was present
The Son was present
The Holy Spirit was present
At creation
All that we made was good
At Creation
You were made in My image
At Creation
I gave you the ability to choose
At Creation
you were given a body and soul
At creation
We walked together in the evening
At Creation
I made provision for all your needs
At Creation
Evil came into the world
At Creation
I promised to protect you
At Creation
I showed you My love and goodness.

MY RESPONSE

Write in your journal and/or share in your facebook/ blog what the word "Image" means to you.

Day 34

SECOND ARTICLE - Redemption

AND IN JESUS CHRIST HIS ONLY SON, OUR LORD

JESUS SPEAKS TO ME OF "LORD"

Today think of Lord.
As you think of Me as Lord, think of our relationship.
As your Lord, I have established My Kingdom
and you are My subject.
As your Lord, I will equip you
for spiritual battle against the evil one.
As your Lord,
listen to My instruction for life's journey.
As your Lord, I lord it over you as your servant
So I wash your feet.
As your Lord,
I will watch over you in times of danger.
As your Lord,
I will provide for you according to your need.
As your Lord,
I will shelter you in the storms of life.
As your Lord,
I will give you direction when you are lost.
As your Lord,
I will provide a community for you to grow in.
As your Lord,
I will provide a place for you to use your gifts.
As your Lord,
I fulfill My promises.

MY RESPONSE

Write in your journal and/or share in your facebook/ blog what the word "Lord" means to you.

Day 35

AND IN JESUS CHRIST HIS ONLY SON, OUR LORD

JESUS SPEAKS TO ME OF "JESUS"

Today think of Jesus.
As Jesus, I know who you are.
As Jesus, I experience what you experience.
As Jesus, I know of your birth for I too have been born.
As Jesus, I know of your joy, for I too have these joys.
As Jesus, I feel your pain, for I too have these pains.
As Jesus, I know of your laughter, for I too laugh.
As Jesus, I feel your broken heart,
for My heart has been broken.
As Jesus, I know your temptation,
for I too have been tempted.
As Jesus, I rejoice with your healing,
for I provided your healing.
As Jesus, I share in your growth,
for I too have grown.
As Jesus, I know of your rejection,
for I too have been rejected.
As Jesus, I know the cross you bear,
for I died on the cross,
As Jesus, I know of death, for I have died.
As Jesus, I know of resurrection
for I have been resurrected.
As Jesus, I sent you My Spirit,
to guide you through life.

MY RESPONSE

Write in your journal and/or share in your facebook/ blog what the word "Jesus" means to you.

Day 36

AND IN JESUS CHRIST HIS ONLY SON, OUR LORD

JESUS SPEAKS TO ME OF "CHRIST"

Today think of Christ.
As Christ, I am the Messiah
to fulfill My promise to you.
As Christ, I am the Anointed One
to bless you with My anointing.
As Christ, I am the Fulfillment of Promise
to show you My faithfulness.
As Christ, I am your Saviour
to save you from sin.
As Christ, I am the High Priest
to intercede for you to the Father.
As Christ I have fulfilled the Law,
so it cannot condemn you.
As Christ, I am your forgiver
so we can be together.
As Christ, I am Grace
to show you the love of the Father.
As Christ, I am the Lamb of God
who takes away the sin of the world.
As Christ, I will return victorious,
defeating the enemy.
As Christ, I will judge the living and the dead,
and vindicate My people.
As Christ, I will establish My Eternal Kingdom,
so we can live together eternally.

MY RESPONSE

Write in your journal and/or share in your facebook/ blog what the word "Christ" means to you.

Day 37

AND IN JESUS CHRIST HIS ONLY SON, OUR LORD

JESUS SPEAKS TO ME OF "SON"

Today think of Son.

As Son, I am loved by My Father,
  As son (daughter) you are loved by My Father.
As Son, I am obedient to My Father,
  As son, you are obedient to My Father.
As Son, I listen to My Father,
  As son, you listen to My Father.
As Son, I trust My Father,
  As son, you trust My Father.
As Son I am blessed by My Father,
  As son, you are blessed by My Father.
As Son, I know what love is,
  As son, you know what love is.
As Son, I know what joy is,
  As son, you know what joy is.
As Son, I know what peace is.
  As son, you know what peace is.
As Son, I know what patience is,
  As son, you know what patience is.
As Son, I know what kindness is,
  As son, you know what kindness is.
As Son, I know what goodness is,
  As son, you know what goodness is.
As Son, I know what faithfulness is,
  As son, you know what faithfulness is.
As Son, I know what gentleness is,
  As son, you know what gentleness is.
As Son, I know what self-control is,
  As son, you know what self-control is.

MY RESPONSE

Write in your journal and/or share in your facebook/blog what the word "Son" means to you.

Day 38

WHO WAS CONCEIVED BY THE HOLY SPIRIT AND BORN OF THE VIRGIN MARY

To conceive means to come to life
When I was conceived by the Holy Spirit
I came to life by the action of God
Not the action of man.

Mary was chosen
Because of her innocence
She had the faith that was necessary
To conceive the Son of God

When I was born of Mary
Mary became the vehicle
For Me to come to earth
And take on Human form.

In the virgin birth
I took on the two Natures
The Divine Nature, being true God
The Human Nature, being true Man.

MY RESPONSE

Write in your journal and/or share in your facebook/ blog what the word "Virgin" means to you.

Day 39

WHO WAS CONCEIVED BY THE HOLY SPIRIT AND BORN OF THE VIRGIN MARY

Being conceived of the Holy Spirit
And Born of Mary
I received both body and Soul
Becoming a human being.

Being conceived by the Holy Spirit
My birth was without sin
For only in this way
I carry the sins of the world.

Being both God and Man
I fulfilled the Heavenly task
To redeem the human race
From the clutches of Sin

In My humanity
I took on the human will
So what I would do
Was My choice alone.

MY RESPONSE

Write in your journal and/or share in your facebook/ blog what the word "Conceived" means to you.

Day 40

SUFFERED UNDER PONTIUS PILATE
WAS CRUCIFIED, DIED, AND WAS BURIED

My suffering was ordained
  by My Father in heaven
My suffering was necessary
  to carry out the work of redemption
My suffering was fulfilled
  for all were lost and condemned
My suffering was carried out
  by Pontius Pilate
My suffering included
  being crucified on the cross
My suffering was innocent
  for I committed no crime
My suffering and death
  won you from sin
My suffering freed you
  from the power of the devil
My suffering and shed blood
  made you My own
My suffering showed My love
  to the whole human race
My suffering made me understand
  the pain in your life
My suffering and burial
  put you in My Kingdom

MY RESPONSE

Write in your journal and/or share in your facebook/ blog what the word "suffering" means to you.

Day 41

HE DESCENDED INTO HELL

In the act of Redemption
My descent into hell
Had to be accomplished
To make the final victory.

My Descent into hell
Was not to suffer for your sins
But to proclaim My victory
Over Sin, Death and Hell.

My descent into Hell
was not to release people
But to preach to the imprisoned
The Way of salvation.

My Descent into Hell
Began My exaltation
Moving from death to life
For the whole human race.

MY RESPONSE

Write in your journal and/or share in your facebook/ blog what the word "Hell" means to you.

Day 42

HE DESCENDED INTO HELL

My descent into Hell
Though My humanity was wounded
I inflicted the death blow
On Satan's demonic power.

My descent into Hell
Comes as a warning
To those unbelievers
Of punishment and eternal doom.

My descent into Hell
Comes as a reminder
To believe in My resurrection
To enter Heaven's home.

MY RESPONSE

Write in your journal and/or share in your facebook/blog what the word "Demonic Power" means to you.

Day 43

THE THIRD DAY HE ROSE AGAIN FROM THE DEAD

I rose from the dead
  to assure victory for all
I rose from the dead
  to conquer all sin
I rose from the dead
  to bring peace to the world
I rose from the dead
  to establish My Kingdom
I rose from the dead
  to have power over death
I rose from the dead
  to change your life
I rose from the dead
  to restore relationships
I rose from the dead
  to reveal the will of My Father
I rose from the dead
  to send my Holy Spirit

MY RESPONSE

Write in your journal and/or share in your facebook/ blog what the words "Rose from the dead" mean to you.

Day 44

HE ASCENDED INTO HEAVEN AND SITS AT THE RIGHT HAND OF GOD THE FATHER ALMIGHTY

I ascended to heaven
  to complete the work of My Father
I ascended to heaven
  in My exaltation of Lordship
I ascended to heaven
  to become the Saviour of the world
I ascended to heaven
  to send the Holy Spirit
I ascended to heaven
  to assure your trip to heaven
I ascended to heaven
  to empower your life
I ascended to heaven
  so you could tell the story
I ascended to heaven
  so the world would change
I ascended to heaven
  to prepare you a home
I ascended to heaven
  with the promise to be with you
I ascended to heaven
  to rule with My Father
I ascended to heaven
  and I promise to come back

MY RESPONSE

Write in your journal and/or share in your facebook/ blog what the word "Ascended" means to you.

Day 45

FROM THERE HE WILL COME TO JUDGE AND LIVING AND THE DEAD.

I am the judge
  of the living and the dead
I am the judge
  so I see what you are doing
I am the judge
  to decide heaven or hell
I am the judge
  and I rule in justice
I am the judge
  and I have mercy and love
I am the judge
  so do not be afraid
I am the judge
  so listen and obey
I am the judge
  so you can have hope

MY RESPONSE

Write in your journal and/or share in your facebook/ blog what the word "Judge" means to you.

Day 46

The Third Article: Sanctification

I BELIEVE IN THE HOLY SPIRIT

The Holy Spirit
  is part of the Trinity
The Holy Spirit
  is sent by Me
The Holy Spirit
  sanctifies your faith
The Holy Spirit
  is your helper in life
The Holy Spirit
  fills you with fruit
The Holy Spirit
  enlightens you with gifts
The Holy Spirit
  empowers you to witness
The Holy Spirit
  protects you from danger
The Holy Spirit
  calls you through the Gospel
The Holy Spirit
  dwells in all believers
The Holy Spirit
  is the interpreter of all truth

MY RESPONSE

Write in your journal and/or share in your facebook/ blog what the word "Sanctification" means to you.

Day 47

THE HOLY CHRISTIAN CHURCH, THE COMMUNION OF SAINTS

The church
 is my Kingdom on earth
The church
 centers on Me
The church
 is called to worship
The church
 is my body in one
The church
 is the communion of saints
The church
 does the work of My Father
The church
 is to pray for each other
The church
 is to pray for the world
The church
 is to study My Word
The church
 is to wait for My coming

MY RESPONSE

Write in your journal and/or share in your facebook/ blog what the word "Saint" means to you.

Day 48

THE FORGIVENESS OF SIN

Forgiveness of sin
  is necessary for salvation
Forgiveness of sin
  is what you received in My death
Forgiveness of sin
  is My Father's gift to you
Forgiveness of sin
  needs to be accepted by you
Forgiveness of sin
  makes one look at yourself
Forgiveness of sin
  helps you fight against the enemy
Forgiveness of sin
  is what you do for others
Forgiveness of sin
  begins the bond of love
Forgiveness of sin
  you both receive and give out
Forgiveness of sin
  needs to come from the heart
Forgiveness of sin
  frees you from bondage.

MY RESPONSE

Write in your journal and/or share in your facebook/ blog what the word "forgiveness" means to you.

Day 49

THE RESURRECTION OF THE BODY

The Resurrection
  is a promise of My Father
The Resurrection
  will take place in the last days
The Resurrection
  is about life after death
The Resurrection
  is about your going to heaven
The Resurrection
  means you will have a new body
The Resurrection
  means the body is united with the soul
The Resurrection
  means you are united with Me

MY RESPONSE

Write in your journal and/or share in your facebook/ blog what the word "Resurrection" means to you.

Day 50

AND THE LIFE EVERLASTING. AMEN

Life everlasting
  was the promise at creation
Life everlasting
  is the promise I made to you
Life everlasting
  comes when you believe in Me
Life everlasting
  is to be in heaven forever
Life everlasting
  can be in heaven or hell
Life everlasting
  is your choice not Mine
Life everlasting
  ends life on earth
Life everlasting
  is a life of celebration
Life everlasting
  is living with Me forever
Life everlasting
  began at your Baptism
Life everlasting
  is life without sin

MY RESPONSE

Write in your journal and/or share in your facebook/ blog what the word "Eternal" means to you.

THE LORD'S PRAYER

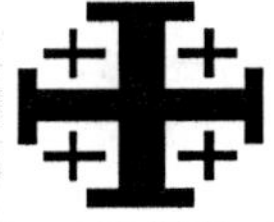

Matthew 6: [5]"And now about prayer. When you pray, don't be like the hypocrites who love to pray publicly on street corners and in the synagogues where everyone can see them. I assure you, that is all the reward they will ever get. [6]But when you pray, go away by yourself, shut the door behind you, and pray to your Father secretly. Then your Father, who knows all secrets, will reward you.

[7]"When you pray, don't babble on and on as people of other religions do. They think their prayers are answered only by repeating their words again and again. [8]Don't be like them, because your Father knows exactly what you need even before you ask him!

[9]Pray like this: Our Father in heaven, may your name be honored. [10] May your Kingdom come soon. May your will be done here on earth, just as it is in heaven. [11] Give us our food for today, [12] and forgive us our sins, just as we have forgiven those who have sinned against us. [13] And don't let us yield to temptation, but deliver us from the evil one.

LUTHER'S SMALL CATECHISM

The Lord's Prayer

Our Father, who art in heaven, hallowed be Thy name, Thy kingdom come, Thy will be done on earth as it is in heaven. Give us this day our daily bread; and forgive us our trespasses as we forgive those who trespass against us; and lead us not into temptation, but deliver us from evil. For Thine is the kingdom and the power and the glory forever and ever. Amen.

The Introduction

Our Father who art in heaven.

What does this mean?

With these words God tenderly invites us to believe that He is our true Father and that we are His true children, so that with all boldness and confidence we may ask Him as dear children ask their dear father.

The First Petition

Hallowed be Thy name.

What does this mean?

God's name is certainly holy in itself, but we pray in this petition that it may be kept holy among us also.

How is God's name kept holy?

God's name is kept holy when the Word of God is taught in its truth and purity, and we, as the children of God, also lead holy lives according to it. Help us to do this, dear Father in heaven! But anyone who teaches or lives contrary to God's Word profanes the name of God among us. Protect us from this, heavenly Father!

The Second Petition

Thy kingdom come.

What does this mean?

The kingdom of God certainly comes by itself without our prayer, but we pray in this petition that it may come to us also.

How does God's kingdom come?

God's kingdom comes when our heavenly Father gives us His Holy Spirit, so that by His grace we believe His Holy Word and lead godly lives here in time and there in eternity.

The Third Petition

Thy will be done on earth as it is in heaven.

What does this mean?

The good and gracious will of God is done even without our prayer, but we pray in this petition that it may be done among us also.

How is God's will done?

God's will is done when he breaks and hinders every evil plan and purpose of the devil, the world, and our sinful nature, which do not want us to hallow God's name or let His kingdom come; and when He strengthens and keeps us firm in His Word and faith until we die. This is His good and gracious will.

The Fourth Petition

Give us this day our daily bread.

What does this mean?

God certainly gives daily bread to everyone without our prayers, even to all evil people, but we pray in this petition that God would lead us to realize this and to receive our daily bread with thanksgiving.

What is meant by daily bread?

Daily bread includes everything that has to do with the support and needs of the body, such as food, drink, clothing, shoes, house, home, land, animals, money, goods, a devout husband or wife, devout children, devout workers, devout and faithful rulers, good government, good weather, peace, health, self control, good reputation, good friends, faithful neighbors, and the like.

The Fifth Petition

And forgive us our trespasses as we forgive those who trespass against us.

What does this mean?

We pray in this petition that our Father in heaven would not look at our sins, or deny our prayer because of them. We are neither worthy of the things for which we pray, nor have we deserved them, but we ask that He would give them all to us by grace, for we daily sin much and surely deserve nothing but punishment. So we too will sincerely forgive and gladly do good to those who sin against us.

The Sixth Petition
And lead us not into temptation.

What does this mean?

God tempts no one. We pray in this petition that God would guard and keep us so that the devil, the world, and our sinful nature may not deceive us or mislead us into false belief, despair, and other great shame and vice. Although we are attacked by these things, we pray that we may finally overcome them and win the victory.

The Seventh Petition
But deliver us from evil.

What does this mean?

We pray in this petition, in summary, that our Father in heaven would rescue us from every evil of body and soul, possessions and reputation, and finally, when our last hour comes, give us a blessed end, and graciously take us from this valley of sorrow to Himself in heaven.

The Conclusion
For thine is the kingdom and the power and the glory forever and ever.* Amen.

What does this mean?

This means that I should be certain that these petitions are pleasing to our Father in heaven, and are heard by Him; for He Himself has commanded us to pray in this way and has promised to hear us. Amen, amen, means, "yes, yes, it shall be so."

Check the Internet
YouTube Lord's Prayer

Day 51

THE LORD'S PRAYER

Our Father, who art in heaven,

JESUS SPEAKS TO ME OF HIS FATHER

When you call Me 'Father'
it warms My heart as it warms your heart.
For you see,
this is what you were meant to call Me
from the beginning of creation.
'Father' speaks of many things:
It speaks of a oneness between Me and you
for we are family.
It speaks of the bond of love between us.
It speaks of a teaching
and learning relationship between us.
It speaks of your willingness to learn from Me.
It speaks of My desire to lead
and protect you under any circumstance.
The word 'Father' says that
My love will always be there
no matter who you are or what you do.
Remember the story of the prodigal son;
My love for the son never faded.

MY RESPONSE

Write in your journal and/or share in your facebook/ blog what the word "Father" means to you.

Day 52

THE LORD'S PRAYER

Our Father, who art in heaven,

JESUS SPEAKS TO ME OF HIS FATHER

When you call me 'Father,'
we both declare that you are My son/daughter.
I am proud to have you as My son/daughter.
'Father' speaks of a God who loves,
For God so loved the world.
I am not a God to be carved on stone
to be placed on a mantel,
for 'Father' says I am a God of relationships.
I am not a God along side other gods,
for 'Father' says I am the only God,
for there can be only one 'Father.'
There are those who find it hard to call Me 'Father,'
because of their earthly fathers.
But remember I have overcome the world.
There are those who find it easy to call Me 'Father,'
and so it should be.

MY RESPONSE

Write in your journal and/or share in your facebook/ blog what the word "Relationship" means to you.

Day 53

THE LORD'S PRAYER

Our Father, who art in heaven

JESUS SPEAKS TO ME OF HIS FATHER

In the word 'Father' the human and the divine
become one.
When you call me 'Father' what you see in me are
tenderness, mercy and forgiveness.
When you call Me 'Father' you will feel
My tender arms surround you to bless you.
To bless means, to say good things.
When you know Me as 'Father'
healing begins to happen in your life,
for you no longer need to fight your own battles.
When you come to know Me as 'Father,'
you then come to know yourself.
When you come to know yourself,
you come to Me in repentance,
therefore seeking forgiveness.
It is then as your 'Father'
I pronounce the absolution on you,
declaring that you are forgiven,
for your sin is paid for by My blood.
When you use the word OUR
it means that you are not alone
on your pilgrimage on earth.
OUR means that you are part of a body
that is united in Me as 'Father.'

MY RESPONSE

Write in your journal and/or share in your facebook/blog what the word "Our" means to you.

Day 54

THE LORD'S PRAYER

Our Father, who art in heaven

JESUS SPEAKS TO ME OF HEAVEN

When you think of heaven
  think of it as a resting place:
  a place where you love to be,
  a place of peace
  a place where you experience My presence.
Heaven is not only a place in the future;
  Heaven is also here and now.
Heaven is a place where you receive love;
  earth is a place where you give love.
If you cannot come to heaven daily
  I cannot give you My love,
  and you have no love to give others.
Heaven is the place
  where you discover who you are
  for I am the only one who can tell you.
When you think of Heaven
  you set your mind on things above
  and not on earthly things.
Do not run from your experience of Heaven,
  even though it may seem fearful at times.

MY RESPONSE

Write in your journal and/or share in your facebook/ blog what the word "Heaven" means to you.

Day 55

THE LORD'S PRAYER

Our Father, who art in heaven

JESUS SPEAKS TO ME OF HEAVEN

Heaven is clothed with glory;
earth is clothed with groaning.
You will always feel the tension
between earth and Heaven,
between temporal and eternal satisfaction.
Heaven is My abiding place
from which I see all the inhabitants of the earth.
Heaven is your abiding place
when we will see each other face to face.
It is in Heaven we walk together;
it is on earth My Spirit enfolds you.
When you focus on Heaven
it will enhance your worship,
it will enhance your evangelism,
it will enhance your purity.
When you go into the world
as one who has experienced Heaven,
you will not go forth as a dependent child,
but as a leader bringing forth
the fruit of My Spirit.
Heaven is not a celestial dream
it is a reality coming true.
Heaven is a fulfillment of My Grace, a free gift to you
paid by My blood on the Cross.

MY RESPONSE

Write in your journal and/or share in your facebook/ blog what the word "Earth" means to you.

Day 56

THE LORD'S PRAYER

Hallowed be Thy name

JESUS SPEAKS TO ME OF HOLINESS

The word HALLOWED means more than HOLY,
for it means MY PRESENCE.
Nothing is holy unless I am present.
My presence makes time, space,
and creation HOLY.
It is not what you do
that makes you HOLY.
My presence makes you HOLY.
Take time to be HOLY
even if the world rushes on.
Spend time with Me in secret
and soak in My HOLY presence.
In the world today
when My presence is denied
you are not in a place of holiness.
In the church today
when My presence is rejected,
it cannot be HOLY.
When you say HALLOWED BE THY NAME
you are calling upon Me to be present
in your time and in your space, now.
When this happens, you become HOLY
because I am present.

MY RESPONSE

Write in your journal and/or share in your facebook/ blog what the word "Holiness" means to you.

Day 57

THE LORD'S PRAYER

Hallowed be Thy name

JESUS SPEAKS TO ME OF HIS NAME

My name is HALLOWED
whenever My word is taught in truth and purity
and you live in harmony with My word.
To HALLOW means to set apart;
when you pray HALLOWED BE THY NAME
you set Me apart, so I set you apart
for you can no longer be of this world.
When you HALLOW and honour My name
miracles will surround you because of My presence.
When you curse My name
destruction surrounds you for I cannot be present.
To HALLOW My name you give praise.
When you give praise it opens the door for Me
to fulfill My promise of being present always.
To HALLOW My name opens the door
to bring healing where there is brokenness.
To HALLOW My name opens the door
for Me to forgive when there is repentance,
and gives you power to forgive others.
Since there is power in My name,
when you pray HALLOWED BE THY NAME
you also receive power.
It is when you pray HALLOWED BE THY NAME
you call upon My HOLY SPIRIT to fill you.

MY RESPONSE

Write in your journal and/or share in your facebook/ blog what the word "Name" means to you.

Day 58

THE LORD'S PRAYER

Thy kingdom come

JESUS SPEAKS TO ME OF HIS KINGDOM

When you pray THY KINGDOM COME,
'THY' says I am
both owner and head of My kingdom.
It is not what you do for Me that brings in My kingdom,
but what I do through you.
When you enter into My kingdom
you leave the world behind;
you acknowledge Me as Lord
and reject the prince of this world.
When you enter into My kingdom you listen to Me.
In My kingdom
you experience the presence of the Holy Spirit.
My kingdom is a garden of prayer,
for in prayer there is fellowship with Me
and fellowship with one another.
My kingdom is the place of Baptism,
baptized in My name and
baptized in the Holy Spirit.
My kingdom is a place of Holy Communion,
communion with Me
and communion with one another.

MY RESPONSE

Write in your journal and/or share in your facebook/ blog what the word "Kingdom" means to you.

Day 59

THE LORD'S PRAYER

Thy kingdom come

JESUS SPEAKS TO ME OF HIS KINGDOM

In My kingdom
you still experience suffering,
suffering of the body,
suffering of relationships, and
suffering because you love Me.
But know this,
My love is greater than any suffering.
In My kingdom
I have established an order of relationships.
The first order is between Me and you.
The second order is between you and family.
The third order is between you and the world.
When you live in My kingdom according to this order
I can then bless you.
In My kingdom I have established:
personal WORSHIP, which is our daily walk together.
the CHURCH to teach you My ways,
the FAMILY to help you express love to one another,
the WORLD to use the gifts I have given to you.

MY RESPONSE

Write in your journal and/or share in your facebook/ blog what the word "Order" means to you.

Day 60

THE LORD'S PRAYER

Thy kingdom come

JESUS SPEAKS TO ME OF HIS KINGDOM

In My kingdom
expect renewal and change
for this is the work of the Holy Spirit.
When you live under My rule in My kingdom
PRAISE of My Name becomes a necessary ingredient,
for it is through praise that you
become refreshed and strengthened to meet the
demands of life.
In My kingdom
your goal should not be to succeed
but to love Me.
My kingdom
is not a time for peace, it is a time for war.
But it is My battle, not your battle.
I have won the victory through My blood.
When you are in My kingdom on earth
you will enter My eternal kingdom.
You cannot enter into My kingdom
unless you are born anew.
This means being born of water and the Spirit.
In My kingdom you are constantly
under the guidance of the Holy Spirit,
for He is the Shepherd that will guide you.

MY RESPONSE

Write in your journal and/or share in your facebook/ blog what the word "Renewal" means to you.

Day 61

THE LORD'S PRAYER

Thy will be done on earth as it is in heaven.

JESUS SPEAKS TO ME OF HIS WILL

My will is known
  when your heart is open to receive it.
As you learn to listen to Me,
  your will is in tune with My will.
The more you focus on Me
  in thought, word and deed,
  the more your life will radiate My will.
I am the creator of all,
  therefore My will is open to all.
  You destroy My will
  by rejecting and destroying My creation.
I willed you and chose you to be Mine
  because I love you.
As a redeemed person you will be under attack,
  therefore it is necessary to live according to My will.
When you do My will, you thwart
  all the attacks and onslaughts of the enemy.
When you do not do My will, it pleases the devil.
  He will use the world and your own flesh to
  entice you.
  Then his will is done on earth.

MY RESPONSE

Write in your journal and/or share in your facebook/ blog what the word "Will" means to you.

Day 62

THE LORD'S PRAYER

Thy will be done on earth as it is in heaven.

JESUS SPEAKS TO ME OF HIS WILL

When My Will is not done, My Kingdom
cannot come and My Name cannot be hallowed.
When you pray
for My will to be done, you will seek TRUTH.
You know My will through creation and
through My written word.
To live My will you must
be transformed by the renewal of your mind.
It is My will that you
hear My voice and harden not your heart.
It is My will that you
follow Me, and live a life of adventure.
It is My will that you
dream great dreams
as I give you the courage to live them.
It is My will that
I be Head of My Body,
as I am King of Kings.
It is My will that
you and I be one
as I and My Father are one.
It is My will that
there be peace among you,
and for you to radiate that peace on earth.

MY RESPONSE

Write in your journal and/or share in your facebook/ blog what the word "Truth" means to you.

Day 63

THE LORD'S PRAYER

Thy will be done on earth as it is in heaven

JESUS SPEAKS TO ME OF HIS WILL

For My will to be done on earth,
I need ambassadors.
I send you forth in the power of the Holy Spirit.
When you pray
"Thy will be done on earth as it is in heaven,"
you will see both death and resurrection.
On earth there must be death
before there can be resurrection.
It is My will that all people experience resurrection.
For My will to be done on earth,
My people must enter into heavenly praise
to be spread throughout the earth.
It is My will that you discover My will and plan
for you, so you will be My fruit in the world.

MY RESPONSE

Write in your journal and/or share in your facebook/ blog what the word "Ambassador" means to you.

Day 64

THE LORD'S PRAYER

Give us this day our daily bread

JESUS SPEAKS TO ME OF DAILY BREAD

Every time you pray
"Give us this day our daily bread"
you are acknowledging My presence
with you on a daily basis.
In this prayer
I am teaching you to trust Me
for your daily needs.
Do not be anxious about tomorrow.
To pray
"Give us this day our daily bread"
means you are always dependent on Me.
You are never self-sufficient.
When you to pray
"Give us this day our daily bread,"
you cannot be selfish with what I give to you.
When you ask Me to give to you
I am teaching you to give to Me
so you can give to others.

MY RESPONSE

Write in your journal what the word "Bread" means to you.

Day 65

THE LORD'S PRAYER

Give us this day our daily bread

JESUS SPEAKS TO ME OF TITHING

When you pray
"Give us this day our daily bread,"
you commit yourself to the tithe.
Giving the tithe is more than a tenth,
it is giving all you have.
It teaches you
how to manage all I have given you.
Giving to Me and giving to others
is being a good steward
of what I have given to you.
In this prayer
I am calling and equipping you
to do something bigger than yourself.
When you pray
"Give us this day our daily bread"
you are asking Me
not only to provide the necessities of life
but also to help you make decisions
in daily living.

MY RESPONSE

Write in your journal and/or share in your facebook/ blog what the word "Tithe" means to you.

Day 66

THE LORD'S PRAYER

Give us this day our daily bread

JESUS SPEAKS TO ME OF BLESSINGS

In this prayer "Give us this day our daily bread,"
you are asking that My peace abide in home
and government, preventing the enemy
to interfere by using division and war.
When you pray "Give us this day our daily bread"
you are asking Me to bestow
My blessing on all people.
In this prayer
you are thanking Me for your daily needs,
and you are also thanking one another.
The greater your awareness of sin
the greater your expression of gratitude.
When you are grateful, you are left in peace
When you are ungrateful, you live in pieces.
When you pray "Give us this day our daily bread,"
I am bestowing upon you
the gifts of the Holy Spirit.
With these gifts you serve each other.
Every time you come to the table of My Supper
I am fulfilling this prayer;
"Give us this day our daily bread."
In My Supper you receive the heavenly bread,
"This is My body."
In "daily bread," you receive My earthly food.

MY RESPONSE

Write in your journal and/or share in your facebook/ blog what the word "Blessings" means to you.

Day 67

THE LORD'S PRAYER

Forgive us our trespasses as we forgive those who trespass against us

JESUS SPEAKS TO ME OF FORGIVENESS

When you pray "Forgive us our sin"
you are seeking forgiveness
from original sin.
The reason I have taught you to pray
'US' in this petition
is because the sin spoken of is corporate.
The sin the first Adam committed reaches all.
The forgiveness the second Adam (Christ)
offers is for all.
At no point are you without My need to forgive,
so you must pray this prayer in every breath.
When you receive My forgiveness,
you come to an understanding
of what it means to be created in My image.
When you receive My forgiveness there is a restoration of the relationship between you and Me.
When you receive My forgiveness you grow in gratitude.
Forgiveness and gratitude are inseparable.
When I died on the cross I paid the price of original sin
so you can receive total forgiveness.
Forgiveness means
the price of your sin is paid for by My blood.

MY RESPONSE

Write in your journal and/or share in your facebook/ blog what the word "Forgiveness" means to you.

Day 68

THE LORD'S PRAYER

Forgive us our trespasses as we forgive those who trespass against

JESUS SPEAKS TO ME OF FORGIVENESS

When you pray
"Forgive us our sin,"
you are declaring that you and the world
are guilty and can then choose forgiveness.
Every time you become conscious
of My presence and holiness, you become conscious of the need for forgiveness.
Forgiveness is necessary
if you are to have a relationship with Me;
therefore seek My forgiveness
through confession and repentance.
Repentance and forgiveness
go hand in hand.
When you receive My forgiveness
you are communing with Me.
When you ask Me to forgive you
you are asking Me
to incarnationally enter into your presence
so you may experience My presence.
When you pray
"Forgive us our sin"
I am declaring to you that you are forgiven.
It is My absolution upon you.

MY RESPONSE

Write in your journal and/or share in your facebook/ blog what the word "Absolution" means to you.

Day 69

THE LORD'S PRAYER

Forgive us our trespasses as we forgive those who trespass against us

JESUS SPEAKS TO ME OF RELATIONSHIPS

"Forgive us our sin"
 is what I do for you;
"As we forgive"
 is what you do for others.
Praying this prayer
 "As we forgive those
 who sin against us."
 means loving unconditionally.
When you pray this prayer
 I am setting you apart,
 for My ways are not the ways of the world.
You cannot keep this prayer on your own.
 so I give you the Holy Spirit to help you.
Receiving My forgiveness bears fruit in your
 forgiving others who sin against you.
Forgiving others
 is a fruit of receiving My forgiveness.
Just as I forgive you always,
 so you must forgive others always.
When you forgive another
 you receive healing.
When you forgive another
 you are setting another free.
When you refuse to forgive another
 you are placing yourself and another in bondage.

MY RESPONSE

Write in your journal and/or share in your facebook/ blog what the word "Fruit" means to you.

Day 70

THE LORD'S PRAYER

Forgive us our trespasses as we forgive those who trespass against us

JESUS SPEAKS TO ME OF BLAME

Forgiveness is not an emotion,
 it is an act of the will.
Offence is a tool of the evil one
 used to break loving relationships.
When you pray this prayer
 I am helping tear down fortified offensive walls
 between you and another
 that have been constructed over time.
You can choose to forgive,
 Or choose not to forgive.
This prayer calls you to repent
 by stopping your blame of others.
 Blaming others tries to justify
 your own action through blindness.
I help you to forgive through My love,
 for forgiveness is a difficult task.
All the fruit of the Holy Spirit are centred on
 the act of forgiveness.
When you withhold forgiveness, you are withholding the fruit of the Holy Spirit from working in you.
At the beginning of each day
 make a decision to pray this prayer,
 "I forgive those
 who will sin against me this day."
 just as I will forgive you throughout your day.

MY RESPONSE

Write in your journal and/or share in your facebook/ blog what the word "Blame" means to you.

Day 71

THE LORD'S PRAYER

Lead us not into temptation

JESUS SPEAKS TO ME OF TEMPTATION

In this prayer
  I am telling you to watch and pray
  so you will not enter into temptation.
When you pray
  "Lead us not into temptation,"
  you are praying that forces beyond your control
  will not have any power over you.
In this prayer
  I am telling you that I do not tempt you.
  It is the Devil, the world and your sinful self
  that tempt you.
When you pray this prayer
  I am allowing you
  to be led to the place of temptation.
  My purpose is to strengthen you,
  to mould and fashion you to maturity.
  I created you with the power to make choices.

MY RESPONSE

Write in your journal and/or share in your facebook/ blog what the word "temptation" means to you.

Day 72

THE LORD'S PRAYER

Lead us not into temptation

JESUS SPEAKS TO ME OF TESTING

In this prayer
  it reminds you that you will daily
  face the seven deadly sins:
  pride, anger,
  envy (jealousy), impurity (lust),
  gluttony, slothfulness, and
  avarice (covetousness).
Trials and temptation
  teach you that you are in spiritual warfare.
Trials and temptation
  strengthen your faith.
When you are led to the place of temptation
  it is a test of faith in yourself
  and a test of your faith in Me.
Both testing and temptation
  will produce in you a quality
  that will stand under pressure.
Do not look at trials and temptation
  from Satan's perspective.
  He is out to destroy you and our friendship.
Look at trials and temptation
  from My perspective
  for through them I desire to show you My love.

MY RESPONSE

Write in your journal and/or share in your facebook/ blog what the word "testing" means to you.

Day 73

THE LORD'S PRAYER

Deliver us from evil

JESUS SPEAKS TO ME OF THE EVIL ONE

When you pray
"But deliver us from evil" (the evil one.)
I give to you a weapon of warfare.
I give divine power to demolish strongholds.
As you live in this world
you are in a constant spiritual battle.
It is the desire of the evil one
to give you comfort in false securities.
These false securities
become strongholds that put you into slavery,
become passions that control your actions,
become habits that bind your thoughts.
When you pray "But deliver us from evil,
I give you wisdom to make the right choices.
I give you discernment to know
the lies of the evil one.
In this prayer, you recognize that I, the 'Lord,' am
your shield, your strength and your stronghold.
When you pray
"But deliver us from evil,"
I free you from any curse
that has been spoken or cast upon you.
In this prayer
I give you My blessing of love and acceptance.

MY RESPONSE

Write in your journal and/or share in your facebook/ blog what the word "Evil" means to you.

Day 74

THE LORD'S PRAYER

Deliver us from evil

JESUS SPEAKS TO ME OF DELIVERANCE

When you pray
  "But deliver us from evil,"
  I will reveal to you through the Holy Spirit
  the lies you are tempted to believe,
  the false strongholds you have chosen to trust.
In this prayer
  you are confessing to Me
  that you have not trusted Me above everything.
When you pray
  "But deliver us from evil,"
  it is a prayer of obedience
  which empowers you to choose the truth
  and reject the lies and strongholds of the evil one.
In this prayer
  you accept My promise
  to protect and guide your ways.
When you pray
  "But deliver us from evil,"
  you are renouncing the sin as it is revealed to you,
asking for My forgiveness.
In this prayer
  I declare to you that you are forgiven,
  for the price of your sin has been paid for
  by My blood.

MY RESPONSE

Write in your journal and/or share in your facebook/ blog what the word "Deliverance" means to you.

Day 75

THE LORD'S PRAYER

For Thine is the kingdom and the power and the glory forever and ever. Amen.

JESUS SPEAKS TO ME OF POWER

When you pray
"For Thine is the Kingdom
and the Power and the Glory
Forever and Ever,"
this is the doxology of My prayer.
The 'Kingdom' is Mine to share.
It is My joy to mould a 'Kingdom'
on earth and in heaven.
It is My delight for you
to experience the fullness of My presence
in My 'Kingdom.'
The 'Kingdom' on earth
is a place to discover who 'I AM.'
The 'Power' is Mine to entrust.
It is My trust that entrusts to you
the 'Power' of the Holy Spirit
to captivate and mould you.
You cannot believe and say 'Jesus is mine'
except by the 'Power' of the Holy Spirit.

MY RESPONSE

Write in your journal and/or share in your facebook/ blog what the word "Power" means to you.

Day 76

THE LORD'S PRAYER

For Thine is the kingdom and the power and the glory forever and ever. Amen.

JESUS SPEAKS TO ME OF GLORY

The 'Glory' is Mine to bless.
It is My love that empowers you
and gives vision of hope for the future.
Knowing My hand of blessing
will transform you into My likeness
so you will reflect My glory.
'Forever' and ever is Mine to enrich.
It is My Divinity
that gives you the sanctity of living forever.
'Forever' is a oneness of relationship
between you and Me.
'Amen' is a word that never ends.
It contains a richness to pass on.
Yes, it shall be so.
It contains the fulfillment
of My promise to you
as you pray My prayer.

MY RESPONSE

Write in your journal and/or share in your facebook/ blog what the word "Glory" means to you.

The Sacrament of Holy Baptism

First

What is Baptism?

Baptism is not just plain water, but it is the water included in God's command and combined with God's word.

Which is that word of God?

Christ our Lord says in the last chapter of Matthew: "Therefore, go and make disciples of all nations, baptizing them in the name of the Father and of the Son and of the Holy Spirit" (Matthew 28:19).

Second

What benefits does Baptism give?

It works forgiveness of sins, rescues from death and the devil, and gives eternal salvation to all who believe this, as the words and promises of God declare.

Which are these words and promises of God?

Christ our Lord says in the last chapter of Mark: "Whoever believes and is baptized will be saved, but whoever does not believe will be condemned" (Mark 16:16).

Third

How can water do such great things?

Certainly not just water, but the word of God in and with the water does these things, along with the faith which trusts this word of God in the water. For without God's word the water is plain water and no Baptism.

But with the word of God it is a Baptism, that is, a life-giving water, rich in grace, and a washing of the new birth in the Holy Spirit, as St. Paul says in Titus, chapter three: "He saved us through the washing of rebirth and renewal by the Holy Spirit, whom He poured out on us generously through Jesus Christ our Savior, so that, having been justified by His grace, we might become heirs having the hope of eternal life. This is a trustworthy saying" (Titus 3:5-8).

Fourth

What does such baptizing with water indicate?

It indicates that the Old Adam in us should by daily contrition and repentance be drowned and die with all sins and evil desires, and that a new man should daily emerge and arise to live before God in righteousness and purity forever.

Where is this written?

St. Paul writes in Romans chapter six: "We were therefore buried with Him through baptism into death in order that, just as Christ was raised from the dead through the glory of the Father, we too may live a new life" (Romans 6:4).

Check the Internet

You tube Baptism

Day 77

When you breathed your first breath
It was Me breathing in you.
For life in the beginning
Was created by Me.

Genesis 2:7 And the LORD God formed a man's body from the dust of the ground and breathed into it the breath of life. And the man became a living person.

You were safe in the womb
Surrounded by water
Developing your organs
Making you unique.

Jeremiah 1:5 "I knew you before I formed you in your mother's womb. Before you were born I set you apart and appointed you as my spokesman to the world."

When you were born
You slid down the canal
To enter the world
Making your first sound.

Luke 2:6 - 7 And while they were there, the time came for her baby to be born. [7]She gave birth to her first child, a son. She wrapped him snugly in strips of cloth and laid him in a manger, because there was no room for them in the village inn.

MY RESPONSE

Write in your journal and/or share in your facebook/ blog what the word "Birth" means to you.

Day 78

Placed in mother's arms
As you sucked on her breast
To get nourishment and strength
For the body to grow.

Luke 2:52 So Jesus grew both in height and in wisdom, and he was loved by God and by all who knew him.

Soon you were brought
To the house of My Father
To be born anew
As is commanded by God.

John 3:5 – 6 [5]Jesus replied, "The truth is, no one can enter the Kingdom of God without being born of water and the Spirit. [6]Humans can reproduce only human life, but the Holy Spirit gives new life from heaven.

You then heard of the time
I was baptized by John
When the Spirit came down
And entered My life.

Mark 1:9 One day Jesus came from Nazareth in Galilee, and he was baptized by John in the Jordan River.

The words came from heaven
As My Father spoke out,
"This is My Son
In whom I am pleased."

Mark 1:10 - 11 And when Jesus came up out of the water, he saw the heavens split open and the Holy Spirit descending like a dove on him. [11]And a voice came from heaven saying, "You are my beloved Son, and I am fully pleased with you."

MY RESPONSE

Write in your journal and/or share in your facebook/ blog what the word "Baptism" means to you.

Day 79

This was done to show
You must be baptized
And enter the water
Sealed by My Spirit.

John 3:5 Jesus replied, "The truth is, no one can enter the Kingdom of God without being born of water and the Spirit.

For then you will hear
The word of My Father
You are My child
In whom I am pleased.

1 John 3:1 See how very much our heavenly Father loves us, for he allows us to be called his children, and we really are!

So now we are one
As we walk through life
Enjoying the challenges
Each day at a time.

Matthew 28:20 Teach these new disciples to obey all the commands I have given you. And be sure of this: I am with you always, even to the end of the age."

MY RESPONSE

Write in your journal and/or share in your facebook/ blog what the word "Child" means to you.

Day 80

In your baptism
The promise is mine
Your obedience is to accept
The gifts of life.

1 Peter 1:3 All honor to the God and Father of our Lord Jesus Christ, for it is by his boundless mercy that God has given us the privilege of being born again. Now we live with a wonderful expectation because Jesus Christ rose again from the dead.

In your baptism
A new life begins
A life steeped in forgiveness
From the original sin.

Psalms 51:5 (NLT) [5] For I was born a sinner— yes, from the moment my mother conceived me.

In your baptism
I pour out My Spirit
Protecting you from danger
And guiding you through life.

Psalms 91:4 He will shield you with his wings. He will shelter you with his feathers. His faithful promises are your armor and protection.

MY RESPONSE

Write in your journal and/or share in your facebook/ blog what the word "Promise" means to you.

Day 81

In your Baptism
I will deliver you from sin
I will deliver you from death
I will deliver you from the devil.

1 Corinthians 10:13 But remember that the temptations that come into your life are no different from what others experience. And God is faithful. He will keep the temptation from becoming so strong that you can't stand up against it. When you are tempted, he will show you a way out so that you will not give in to it.

In your Baptism
I clean your past
By removing the strongholds
That control your life.

2 Corinthians 10:4 We use God's mighty weapons, not mere worldly weapons, to knock down the Devil's strongholds.

In your Baptism
I seal your commitment
That you accept My death
And My shed Blood.

Joshua 24:15 [15]But if you are unwilling to serve the LORD, then choose today whom you will serve. Would you prefer the gods your ancestors served beyond the Euphrates? Or will it be the gods of the Amorites in whose land you now live? But as for me and my family, we will serve the LORD."

MY RESPONSE

Write in your journal and/or share in your facebook/ blog what the word "Deliver" means to you.

Day 82

In your Baptism
You must accept by faith
The miracle that takes place
In water and the Word.

Jeremiah 15:16 Your words are what sustain me. They bring me great joy and are my heart's delight, for I bear your name, O LORD God Almighty.

On the day you were Baptized
It shall not be forgotten
To be renewed every day
Until life's end.

Deuteronomy 6:7 Repeat them again and again to your children. Talk about them when you are at home and when you are away on a journey, when you are lying down and when you are getting up again.

In your Baptism
I give you My blessing
In the name of the Father
The Son and the Holy Spirit.

2 Samuel 7:28 - 29 For you are God, O Sovereign LORD.
Your words are truth, and you have promised these good
things to me, your servant. 29And now, may it please you to
bless me and my family so that our dynasty may continue
forever before you. For when you grant a blessing to your
servant, O Sovereign LORD, it is an eternal blessing!"

MY RESPONSE

Write in your journal and/or share in your facebook/ blog what the word "Faith" means to you.

The Sacrament of the Altar

What is the Sacrament of the Altar?

It is the true body and blood of our Lord Jesus Christ under the bread and wine, instituted by Christ Himself for us Christians to eat and to drink.

Where is this written?

The holy Evangelists Matthew, Mark, Luke and St. Paul write: Our Lord Jesus Christ, on the night when He was betrayed, took bread, and when He had given thanks, He broke it and gave it to the disciples and said: "Take, eat; this is My body, which is given for you. This do in remembrance of Me." In the same way also he took the cup after supper, and when He had given thanks, He gave it to them, saying, "Drink of it, all of you; this cup is the new testament in My blood, which is shed for you for the forgiveness of sins. This do, as often as you drink it, in remembrance of Me."

What is the benefit of this eating and drinking?

These words, "Given and shed for you for the forgiveness of sins," shows us that in the Sacrament forgiveness of sins, life, and salvation are given us through these words. For where there is forgiveness of sins, there is also life and salvation.

How can bodily eating and drinking do such great things?

Certainly not just eating and drinking do these things, but the words written here: "Given and shed for you for the forgiveness of sins." These words, along with the bodily eating and drinking, are the main thing in the Sacrament. Whoever believes these words has exactly what they say: "forgiveness of sins."

Who receives this sacrament worthily?

Fasting and bodily preparation are certainly fine outward training. But that person is truly worthy and well prepared who has faith in these words: "Given and shed for you for the forgiveness of sins." But anyone who does not believe these words or doubts them is unworthy and unprepared, for the words "for you" require all hearts to believe.

Check the Internet

Youtube Holy Communion

Day 83

When you gather with Me
Around My table
You come to receive
And not to give.

Remember the past
Of the Passover lamb.
In bondage you were
Under the shackles of sin.

The Lamb's blood was shed
To be saved from the curse.
For death was close by
To strike its dark hand.

Death passed over the one
Who received the true blood
For the Passover lamb
Was a picture of Me.

So when you come to the table
Remember the Passover
And be freed from the shackles,
That sin wants to hold.

MY RESPONSE

Write in your journal and/or share in your facebook/ blog what the word "Sacrament" means to you.

Day 84

This is the time
That My blood is being shed
So come as you are
With nothing to hide.

Come to My table
With joy in your head
As you celebrate My presence
At the table we meet.

Come to My table
With healing in mind
As I reach out and touch
The place that is hurt.

Come to My table
With forgiveness in mind.
As you hear My word,
"For the forgiveness of sin."

Come to My table
With relationships broken.
As I place My arms
And bring you close in.

Come to My table
when you are feeling alone
As I reach out and take
the hand hanging limp.

MY RESPONSE

Write in your journal and/or share in your facebook/ blog what the word "Table" means to you.

Day 85

Remember the present
As I speak the words
My body is broken
My blood is shed.

On this night
I take the bread
For this is My body
I break for you.

When I break My body
I break the curse
That comes on all men
Who till the earth.

When I break My body
I break the curse
That came on all women
In giving new birth.

When I break My body
I break the curse
That came on all creation
Because of sin's judgment.

When you receive My body
I restore you to life.
To live in My presence
In oneness again.

MY RESPONSE
Write in your journal and/or share in your facebook/ blog what the word "Body" means to you.

Day 86

On this night
I take the cup
That contains My blood
That is shed for you.

When you receive My Blood
Your life is restored
In a new creation
Of the Tree of Life.

When you receive My blood
You hear My word
That you are forgiven
And you are free.

When you receive My blood
I give you new vision
With purpose to live
A life in My plan.

When you receive My blood
I give you My Spirit
That is full of good fruit
And gifts galore.

When you receive My blood
You're ready for the future
For I am coming back
To receive you again.

MY RESPONSE

Write in your journal and/or share in your facebook/ blog what the word "Blood" means to you.

Day 87

Remember the future
As you come to My table
For here you live out
What I'm giving to you.

I want you to tell
The world what I've done
So they can receive
My blessing as well.

I am depending on you
For you are My voice
To speak forth My love
For all to see.

I am depending on you
For you are My hands
To reach out and touch
The ones that are hurt.

I am depending on you
For you are My ears
For I need to hear
From the across the earth.

I am depending on you
For you are My feet
For I need to go
Where people do meet.

MY RESPONSE

Write in your journal and/or share in your facebook/ blog what the word "Future" means to you.

Day 88

I am depending on you
For you are My heart
And from your heart
People see Me.

When people see Me
They will see My body
When people receive Me
Their brokenness is healed.

When people see Me
They will see My shed blood
When people receive Me
Their life is restored.

So when you go out
Exit the world
For that is the mission
You now love to keep.

MY RESPONSE

Write in your journal and/or share in your facebook/ blog what the word "Mission" means to you.

Christian Questions with Their Answers

Prepared by Dr. Martin Luther for those who intend to go to the Sacrament

After confession and instruction in the Ten Commandments, the Creed, the Lord's Prayer, and the Sacraments of Baptism and the Lord's Supper, the pastor may ask, or Christians may ask themselves these questions:

1. Do you believe that you are a sinner?
Yes, I believe it. I am a sinner.

2. How do you know this?
From the Ten Commandments, which I have not kept.

3. Are you sorry for your sins?
Yes, I am sorry that I have sinned against God.

4. What have you deserved from God because of your sins?
His wrath and displeasure, temporal death, and eternal damnation. See Romans 6:21, 23.

5. Do you hope to be saved?
Yes, that is my hope.

6. In whom then do you trust?
In my dear Lord Jesus Christ.

7. Who is Christ?
The Son of God, true God and man.

8. How many Gods are there?
Only one, but there are three persons: Father, Son, and Holy Spirit.

9. What has Christ done for you that you trust in Him?
He died for me and shed His blood for me on the cross for the forgiveness of sins.

10. Did the Father also die for you?
He did not. The Father is God only, as is the Holy Spirit; but the Son is both true God and true man. He died for me and shed his blood for me.

11. How do you know this?

From the holy Gospel, from the words instituting the Sacrament, and by His body and blood given me as a pledge in the Sacrament.

12. What are the Words of Institution?

Our Lord Jesus Christ, on the night when He was betrayed, took bread and when He had given thanks, He broke it and gave it to the disciples and said: "Take eat; this is My body, which is given for you. This do in remembrance of Me." In the same way also He took the cup after supper, and when He had given thanks, He gave it to them, saying: "Drink of it, all of you; this cup is the new testament in My blood, which is shed for you for the forgiveness of sins. This do, as often as you drink it, in remembrance of Me."

13. Do you believe, then, that the true body and blood of Christ are in the Sacrament?

Yes, I believe it.

14. What convinces you to believe this?

The word of Christ: Take, eat, this is My body; drink of it, all of you, this is My blood.

15. What should we do when we eat His body and drink His blood, and in this way receive His pledge?

We should remember and proclaim His death and the shedding of His blood, as He taught us: This do, as often as you drink it, in remembrance of Me.

16. Why should we remember and proclaim His death?

First, so that we may learn to believe that no creature could make satisfaction for our sins.

Only Christ, true God and man, could do that. Second, so we may learn to be horrified by our sins, and to regard them as very serious. Third, so we may find joy and comfort in Christ alone, and through faith in Him be saved.

17. What motivated Christ to die and make full payment for your sins?

His great love for His Father and for me and other sinners, as it is written in John 14; Romans 5; Galatians 2 and Ephesians 5.

18. Finally, why do you wish to go to the Sacrament?

That I may learn to believe that Christ, out of great love, died for my sin, and also learn from Him to love God and my neighbor.

19. What should admonish and encourage a Christian to receive the Sacrament frequently?

First, both the command and the promise of Christ the Lord. Second, his own pressing need, because of which the command, encouragement, and promise are given.

20. But what should you do if you are not aware of this need and have no hunger and thirst for the Sacrament?

To such a person no better advice can be given than this: first, he should touch his body to see if he still has flesh and blood. Then he should believe what the Scriptures say of it in Galatians 5 and Romans 7. Second, he should look around to see whether he is still in the world, and remember that there will be no lack of sin and trouble, as the Scriptures say in John 15-16 and in 1 John 2 and 5. Third, he will certainly have the devil also around him, who with his lying and murdering day and night will let him have no peace, within or without, as the Scriptures picture him in John 8 and 16; 1 Peter 5; Ephesians 6; and 2 Timothy 2.

Confession

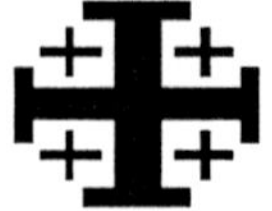

How Christians should be taught to confess.

What is confession?
Confession has two parts. First, that we confess our sins, and second, that we receive absolution, that is, forgiveness, from the pastor as from God Himself, not doubting, but firmly believing that by it our sins are forgiven before God in heaven.

What sins should we confess?
Before God we should plead guilty of all sins, even those we are not aware of, as we do in the Lord's Prayer; but before the pastor we should confess only those sins which we know and feel in our hearts.

Which are these?
Consider your place in life according to the Ten Commandments: Are you a father, mother, son, daughter, husband, wife, or worker? Have you been disobedient, unfaithful, or lazy? Have you been hot-tempered, rude, or quarrelsome? Have you hurt someone by your words or deeds? Have you stolen, been negligent, wasted anything, or done any harm?

A Short Form of Confession
[Luther intended the following form to serve as an example of private confession.

The penitent says:
Dear confessor, I ask you please to hear my confession and to pronounce forgiveness in order to fulfill God's will. I, a poor sinner, plead guilty before God of all sins. In particular I confess before you that as a servant, maid, etc., I, sad to say, serve my master unfaithfully, for in this and that I have not done what I was told to do.

I have made him angry and caused him to curse. I have been negligent and allowed damage to be done. I have also been offensive in words and deeds. I have quarreled with my peers. I have grumbled about the lady of the house and cursed her. I am sorry for all of this and I ask for grace. I want to do better.

A master or lady of the house may say:
In particular I confess before you that I have not faithfully guided my children, servants, and wife to the glory of God. I have cursed. I have set a bad example by indecent words and deeds. I have hurt my neighbor and spoken evil of him. I have overcharged, sold inferior merchandise, and given less than was paid for.
[Let the penitent confess whatever else he has done against God's commandments and his
own position].
If, however, someone does not find himself burdened with these or greater sins, he should not trouble himself or search for or invent other sins, and thereby make confession a torture. Instead, he should mention one or two that he knows: In particular I confess that I have cursed; I have used improper words; I have neglected this or that, etc. Let that be enough. But if you know of none at all (which hardly seems possible), then mention none in particular, but receive the forgiveness upon the general confession which you make to God before the confessor.

Then the confessor shall say:
God be merciful to you and strengthen your faith. Amen.

Furthermore:
Do you believe that my forgiveness is God's forgiveness? Yes, dear confessor.

Then let him say:
Let it be done for you as you believe. And I, by the command of our Lord Jesus Christ, forgive you your sins in the name of the Father and of the Son and of the Holy Spirit. Amen. Go in peace. A confessor will know additional passages with which to comfort and to strengthen

the faith of those who have great burdens of conscience or are sorrowful and distressed. This is intended only as a general form of confession.

What is the Office of the Keys?*

The Office of the Keys is that special authority which Christ has given to His church on earth to forgive the sins of repentant sinners, but to withhold forgiveness from the unrepentant as long
as they do not repent.

Where is this written?*

This is what St. John the Evangelist writes in chapter twenty: The Lord Jesus breathed on His disciples and said, 'Receive the Holy Spirit. If you forgive anyone his sins, they are forgiven; if you do not forgive them, they are not forgiven' (John 20:22-23).

What do you believe according to these words?*

I believe that when the called ministers of Christ deal with us by His divine command, in particular when they exclude openly unrepentant sinners from the Christian congregation and absolve those who repent of their sins and want to do better, this is just as valid and certain, even in heaven, as if Christ our dear Lord dealt with us Himself.

Day 89

PRAYER FOR PURIFICATION

From HATE to LOVE

Lord,
From your words I see that I am not to hate anyone.
That's hard at times
Help me today
  to love the person I hate,
  to love the person I don't like.
  to love the person I disagree with.
Forgive me for talking about people
  in such a way that it hurts them.
Purify my thoughts Lord Jesus
  by taking away all hatred and resentment
  and replace it with your love.
I want so much to be close to You in my daily walk.
  I know it is not possible when I hate.
I want so much to love those who are close to me.
  I know love suffers when I hate,
  or am resentful toward others.
I call upon you, Lord,
  to help me overcome this sin.
Amen.
THE LORD'S PRAYER

MY RESPONSE

Write in your journal and/or share in your facebook/ blog what the word "Hate" means to you.

Day 90

PRAYER FOR PURIFICATION

From DEPRESSION to JOY

Lord, Jesus
Forgive me for not trusting in You.
In your word
  You promise to be with me in my feelings of
  depression, anxiety, loneliness and fear.
I claim this promise for myself right NOW.
I feel so good to know
  I will never be alone again.
You promise that things will never get so bad
  that I cannot handle it.
You will give to me the strength I need.
Lord, increase my faith, and my praise of You.
Lord, give me something to live for, some direction.
Help me to give my problems to you and let them go.
Help me to rejoice when others succeed.
Help me to count the blessings in my life today.
  1______2______3______4______5______
I feel good as I claim Your joy, Lord.
Thank you. Amen.
THE LORD'S PRAYER

MY RESPONSE

Write in your journal and/or share in your facebook/ blog what the word "Depression" means to you.

Day 91

PRAYER FOR PURIFICATION

From STRIFE to PEACE

Lord Jesus,
You have come to bring peace on earth.
I am part of this world
and I need the peace that you have come to bring.
I know I can have this peace
when I accept you as my Lord and Saviour.
You have said,
"Peace I leave with you."
I accept you now as Lord of my life.
Forgive me for taking on so much
that in my anxiety I lose your PEACE.
Forgive me for being selfish,
not caring for others so I lose your PEACE
Forgive me for feeding my mind with evil
by what I read, hear, or see, so I lose your PEACE.
Forgive me for being angry at people I love
running them down, so I lose your PEACE.
Forgive me for cursing those
who I feel have caused division and strife.
Help me to bless others
even if I disagree with them.
Help me to realize your Peace can be with me
even when things don't go right.
Help me to have your Peace
even in strife and conflict.
Help me to share your PEACE
with all I know and meet. Amen
THE LORD'S PRAYER

MY RESPONSE

Write in your journal and/or share in your facebook/ blog what the word "Strife" means to you.

Day 92

PRAYER FOR PURIFICATION

From IMPATIENCE to PATIENCE

Lord Jesus,
I don't want to be impatient with You or with others.
Forgive me for being so impatient
  with the one I love,
  with my children,
  with my parents,
  with those I meet,
  with those in authority,
  and with You Lord.
When I look into your Word
  I see how patient you were with people
  even if they rejected you many times.
You are so patient with me
  even in my impatience.
I need Your patience.
Give me Your patience
  as I serve those I love.
Give me Your patience
  as I help those in need.
Give me You patience
  as I wait for Your time.
Holy Spirit
  teach me to be patient in my daily walk.
Amen.
THE LORD'S PRAYER

MY RESPONSE
Write in your journal and/or share in your facebook/ blog what the word "Impatient" means to you.

Day 93

PRAYER FOR PURIFICATION

From JEALOUSY to KINDNESS

Lord Jesus,
take away my jealousy,
for I see what it does to me,
and to my relationship to others, and to You.
Replace my jealousy with kindness.
Rather than being jealous,
I desire to be happy about the success of others.
I want to be pleased when others get attention.
I want to be thankful when others receive awards.
May the Holy Spirit control my thoughts and actions
so that kindness is a natural part of my life.
I pray Lord,
that through my acts of kindness
others will be better people.
May the kindness I show
be a small sample
of the kindness you have shown me.
Thank you, Lord Jesus
for being so kind.
THE LORD'S PRAYER

MY RESPONSE

Write in your journal and/or share in your facebook/ blog what the word "Jealousy" means to you.

Day 94

PRAYER OF PURIFICATION

From EVIL to GOODNESS

Lord Jesus,
when You told people to be good
  you told them to repent.
I come before you now,
  reporting and repenting
  of all the evil I do and think.
Purify me Lord,
  so my inner thoughts become Holy,
  so my actions become acts of goodness,
  so my desire is obedient to your leading.
I want so much
  for my will to become Your will,
for my thoughts to become Your thoughts,
  for my deeds to become Your deeds,
  for my goodness to become Your goodness.
I realize this is possible
  only when the Holy Spirit dwells in my body
  so my body becomes your temple.
May my lips
  only speak of Your goodness.
May my hands
  become tools of Your goodness.
May my feet lead me away from evil
  as I walk in Your footprints.
Thank You Lord. Amen

THE LORD'S PRAYER

MY RESPONSE

Write in your journal and/or share in your facebook/ blog what the word "Evil" means to you.

Day 95

PRAYER FOR PURIFICATION

From UNRELIABLE to FAITHFULNESS

Lord Jesus,
I see You are so faithful and Your Love being so vast,
even when others are unfaithful to you.
Forgive me Lord,
for being unfaithful to You,
and unreliable to others.
May the Holy Spirit
Help me to be faithful in prayer,
and constant in reading your Word.
Help me to be enduring
when there is a task before me.
Help me to be loyal to my loved ones.
Help me to be trustworthy
to those I work with and work for.
Help me to be truthful
in times of testing.
Help me to be dependable
so I will be given responsibility.
Help me to be obedient
to those in authority.
Help me to be honest in what I do
and not cheat to get approval.
Help me Lord,
to be faithful to You
so that it will reflect in my daily life
and I can be Your faithful servant.
Amen.
THE LORD'S PRAYER

MY RESPONSE

Write in your journal and/or share in your facebook/ blog what the word "Unreliable" means to you.

Day 96

PRAYER FOR PURIFICATION

From SELFISHNESS to GENTLENESS

Lord Jesus,
I see now that Gentleness, Meekness, and Humility
 is giving you the praise and glory
 rather than taking it for myself.
Forgive me Lord for being self-centered
 by wanting to put myself on the throne of my life.
Forgive me for striving for my own rights
 at the expense of hurting others.
Forgive me for proudly receiving compliments
 in order to boost my own ego.
Forgive me for focusing on complaining
 rather than enjoying the time at hand.
Forgive me striving for success
 that will hurt and run others down
Forgive me for pride
 that leads to self glorification,
 at the expense of glorifying You Lord.
Lord, help me to show your Spirit of Gentleness
 as I relate to others who are hurting.
To show Your Spirit of Meekness
 as I help whose who are weak.
To show Your Spirit of Humility in all that I do.
To God be the glory. Amen.

THE LORD'S PRAYER

MY RESPONSE

Write in your journal and/or share in your facebook/ blog what the word "Selfish" means to you.

Day 97

PRAYER FOR PURIFICATION

From NO DISCIPLINE to SELF CONTROL

Lord Jesus,
I realize that I am a slave to whatever controls me.
Forgive me Lord,
For committing myself to You
  but making little effort to control my ways.
For not controlling
  my thoughts and desires,
  my time and money,
  my entertainment and work.
For allowing outside influences such as
  food, drink, bad habits, ______,______,______
  to take over my life so that I lose control.
Help me to realize that to be self-controlled
  I need to be Christ-controlled.
To be Christ-Controlled
  I need to give the Holy Spirit
  permission to take over my life.
Help me Lord
  to get rid of the habits that control me,
  so I may be a better influence to others.
Thank you, Lord
  for helping me to be Christ – Controlled.
Amen

MY RESPONSE

Write in your journal and/or share in your facebook/ blog what the word "No Discipline" means to you.

THE FRUIT OF THE HOLY SPIRIT

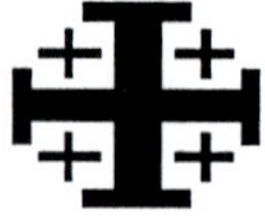

Galatians 5: [16]So I advise you to **live according to your new life in the Holy Spirit.** Then you won't be doing what your sinful nature craves. [17]The old sinful nature loves to do evil, which is just opposite from what the Holy Spirit wants. And the Spirit gives us desires that are opposite from what the sinful nature desires. These two forces are constantly fighting each other, and your choices are never free from this conflict. [18]But when you are directed by the Holy Spirit, you are no longer subject to the law.

[19]When you follow the **desires of your sinful nature,** your lives will produce these evil results: sexual immorality, impure thoughts, eagerness for lustful pleasure, [20]idolatry, participation in demonic activities, hostility, quarreling, jealousy, outbursts of anger, selfish ambition, divisions, the feeling that everyone is wrong except those in your own little group, [21]envy, drunkenness, wild parties, and other kinds of sin. Let me tell you again, as I have before, that anyone living that sort of life will not inherit the Kingdom of God.

[22]But when the Holy Spirit controls our lives, he will produce this kind of fruit in us: love, joy, peace, patience, kindness, goodness, faithfulness, [23]gentleness, and self-control.

Check the Internet
YouTube Fruit of the Spirit

Day 98

FRUIT OF THE SPIRIT

JESUS SPEAKS TO ME OF LOVE

The love that I give
is the fruit of My Holy Spirit.
It is My Divine Love
that is expressed in human behavior.
Greater love has no one than this,
that he lay down his life for another.
This is the greatest expression of My Divine Love,
for I gave My life for you.
My Divine Love reaches out to all
regardless of what a person has done.
My Divine Love forgives all
no matter how one has been hurt.
My Divine Love helps all
regardless of who they are.
When you receive My Divine Love
it takes all bitter roots of hatred away
and sets you free.
My Divine Love puts a protection around you
so that the enemy cannot turn love into lust.
The love that I give through My Spirit
is an everlasting love.

MY RESPONSE

Write in your journal and/or share in your facebook/ blog what the word "Love" means to you.

Day 99

FRUIT OF THE SPIRIT

JESUS SPEAKS TO ME OF LOVE

Once you have received My Divine Love
I will never take it from you.
You may choose to reject it
but I will always reach out with My Divine Love.
My Divine Love in My Spirit
gives you the ability to choose.
This is the greatest gift I can give to you.
You can choose to accept Me or reject Me.
You can choose to do good or do evil.
You can choose to help someone or hurt someone.
You can choose to love or to hate.
Being able to choose love
sets you free to be able to love.
Living My Divine Love
becomes a natural instinct
and becomes a part of you as it is a part of Me.
So I abide in you and you abide in Me.
My Divine Love in My Spirit
is not so much an action as it is an intuition.
You receive it and do it without your awareness.
When you receive My Spirit
you receive the fruit of My Divine Love.

MY RESPONSE

Write in your journal and/or share in your facebook/ blog what the word "Choice" means to you.

Day 100

FRUIT OF THE SPIRIT

JESUS SPEAKS TO ME OF JOY

The Joy that I give
    is the fruit of My Holy Spirit
It is My Divine Joy.
In My Divine Joy
    you receive strength,
    for the Joy of the Lord is my strength.
It is because of Divine Joy
    that you are able to give praise in My name.
It is the enemy
    that feeds you with depression.
My Divine Joy
    gives you the strength to overcome depression.
It is the enemy
    that brings on sickness and brokenness.
My Divine Joy
    brings healing of body, soul and spirit.
It is the enemy
    that breaks the family.
My Divine Joy
    heals relations between people.
It is the enemy
    that makes one focus
    on sufferings and hardships,
    bringing hopelessness and despair.

MY RESPONSE

Write in your journal and/or share in your facebook/ blog what the word "Joy" means to you.

Day 101

FRUIT OF THE SPIRIT

JESUS SPEAKS TO ME OF JOY

My Divine Joy
brings joy into your life in spite of suffering,
brings celebration instead of hopelessness,
brings hope instead of despair.
My Divine Joy
helps you see and live the positive
rather than the negative,
helps you see good in yourself and others,
helps you laugh at yourself and with others.
My Divine Joy
gives you a healthy motivation for life,
gives a sense of sheer gratitude and thankfulness,
gives you a smiling heart which finds expression
on your face.
My Divine Joy
is not so much an action as it is an intuition.
You receive it and do it without your awareness
when you receive My Spirit.
My Divine Joy
draws you to Me in an expression of continuous
worship.

MY RESPONSE

Write in your journal and/or share in your facebook/ blog what the word "Celebration" means to you.

Day 102

FRUIT OF THE SPIRIT

JESUS SPEAKS TO ME OF PEACE

The Peace that I give
    is the fruit of My Holy Spirit.
It is My Divine Peace.
My Divine Peace
    is a peace you will never understand,
    for it 'surpasses understanding.'
My Divine Peace
    begins in your heart
    and then reaches out through all your senses.
You speak
    words of peace to others.
You reach out and touch
    bringing healing.
Your eyes
    bring peace as they rest on others.
You hear
    the pain of others and desire to bring peace.
You smell
    the foul presence of the enemy.
Your presence
    in the midst of others brings comfort.

MY RESPONSE

Write in your journal and/or share in your facebook/ blog what the word "Peace" means to you.

Day 103

FRUIT OF THE SPIRIT

JESUS SPEAKS TO ME OF PEACE

When I share My Divine Peace
I share My Blessing.
When you share My Divine Peace
you give My Blessing.
My Divine Peace in My Spirit
is not a passive peace but an aggressive peace,
for My Divine Peace cannot tolerate injustice.
My Divine Peace
equips you with My full armor
so that you are ready for battle.
In battle, your motive and desire
is to bring My Divine Peace.
My Divine Peace
gives you strength and courage
to take on the wars of the enemy.
My Divine Peace
gives you confidence that the battles in life
will be won
because I am the Victor.
My Divine Peace
places within you the ultimate desire
to be near to Me as I am near to you.

MY RESPONSE

Write in your journal and/or share in your facebook/ blog what the word "aggression" means to you.

Day 104

FRUIT OF THE SPIRIT

JESUS SPEAKS TO ME OF PATIENCE

The Patience that I give
    is the fruit of My Holy Spirit.
It is My Divine Patience.
My Divine Patience
    puts you into My time zone
    so that you do not worry.
My Divine Patience
    removes the anxieties of life
    so that you can learn to relax.
My Divine Patience
    helps you enjoy My presence
    and your walk with Me.
My Divine Patience
    makes Me patient with you
    so I expect you to be patient with others.
My Divine Patience
    renews your strength and your courage
    as you "wait upon the Lord."
    You will soar on wings like eagles.
In fulfilling My Divine Patience
    you begin to see the fulfillment of My promises.

MY RESPONSE
Write in your journal and/or share in your facebook/ blog what the word "Patience" means to you.

Day 105

FRUIT OF THE SPIRIT

JESUS SPEAKS TO ME OF PATIENCE

My Divine Patience
opens the door of opportunity
as you listen and do My will.
As you experience My Divine Patience
It gives Me time to restore your health.
For then the pressures of life
will not weigh you down and afflict you.
Encountering impatience and anger from others
provides an opportunity
to express My Divine Patience.
My Divine Patience
replaces haughty pride
that leads to the destruction of My Divine Love.
My Divine Patience
restores relationships by removing impatience
and anger.
My Divine Patience
helps you focus on the future of My return.
My Divine Patience
is not so much an action as it is an intuition.
It is a gift from Me to you.
Then My Divine Patience
becomes part of who you are.

MY RESPONSE

Write in your journal and/or share in your facebook/ blog what the word "Opportunity" means to you.

Day 106

FRUIT OF THE SPIRIT

JESUS SPEAKS TO ME OF KINDNESS

The Kindness that I give
is the fruit of My Holy Spirit.
It is My Divine Kindness.
My Divine Kindness
is My servant gift to you.
In Divine Kindness
you reach out to others
with no expectation of gain or return.
It is My Divine Kindness
that removes human behaviors
that center on self:
selfishness, jealousy and pride.
In receiving My Divine Kindness
you will have the desire to
lift others up rather than yourself.
My Divine Kindness
will mean sacrifice,
for often it will not be accepted by others.
Through this I will raise you up
for through Divine Kindness
you raise Me up.

MY RESPONSE

Write in your journal and/or share in your facebook/ blog what the word "Kindness" means to you.

Day 107

FRUIT OF THE SPIRIT

JESUS SPEAKS TO ME OF KINDNESS

My Divine Kindness
will help you express words of kindness
that will touch
the hearts of people.
Through this lives will be changed
and people will be drawn into
My presence.
My Divine Kindness
is the fruit in which the gift of exhortation
operates.
As I encourage you,
so you will encourage others.
My Divine Kindness
will help you rejoice
as you see others being blessed.
By accepting the fruit of My Divine Kindness
others will be drawn to you
for they will see My love in you.
My Divine Kindness
is an intuitive fruit through which
you will do random acts of kindness.

MY RESPONSE

Write in your journal and/or share in your facebook/ blog what the word "Touch" means to you.

Day 108

FRUIT OF THE SPIRIT

JESUS SPEAKS TO ME OF GOODNESS

The Goodness that I give
    is the fruit of My Holy Spirit.
It is My Divine Goodness.
In My Divine Goodness
    you are able to discern
    good from evil.
In My Divine Goodness
You see the difference between love and hate,
    but you choose love.
You see the difference between joy and depression,
    but you choose joy.
You see the difference between peace and war,
    but you choose peace.
You see the difference between patience and
  violence,
    but you choose patience.
You see the difference between kindness and anger,
  but you choose kindness.
You see the difference between goodness and evil,
  but you choose goodness.

MY RESPONSE

Write in your journal and/or share in your facebook/ blog what the word "Goodness" means to you.

Day 109

FRUIT OF THE SPIRIT

JESUS SPEAKS TO ME OF GOODNESS

In My Divine Goodness
You see the difference between
faithfulness and faithlessness,
but you choose faithfulness.
You see the difference between self-control
and uncontrolled behavior,
but you choose self-control.
My Divine Goodness
not only helps you to see the difference
but gives you the strength and the
confidence to live your choice.
In My Divine Goodness
you will often feel alone
because it is in opposition to the
fruit of the flesh.
Know this, 'I am always with you.'
My Divine Goodness
will give you a boldness
to stand up for that which is good,
and thus make this world a better
and safer place to live.

MY RESPONSE

Write in your journal and/or share in your facebook/ blog what the word "Confidence" means to you.

Day 110

FRUIT OF THE SPIRIT

JESUS SPEAKS TO ME OF FAITHFULNESS

The Faithfulness that I give
is the fruit of My Holy Spirit.
It is My Divine Faithfulness.
You discover my Divine Faithfulness
only in terms of relationships
For My Divine Faithfulness
comes out of obedience.
My Divine Faithfulness
is another expression of My love
toward you
and your love toward Me.
My Divine Faithfulness
shows itself in many ways in your life:
by listening with a glad and sincere heart,
by sharing My abundance with others,
by learning the treasures of life,
by fulfilling your promises to Me.

MY RESPONSE

Write in your journal and/or share in your facebook/ blog what the word "Faithfulness" means to you.

Day 111

FRUIT OF THE SPIRIT

JESUS SPEAKS TO ME OF FAITHFULNESS

It is My Divine Faithfulness
that gives you the courage
to be obedient to Me
even if you do not understand
the significance of My command.
My Divine Faithfulness
will bless you with ambition,
will bless you with vision,
will bless you with action.
My Divine Faithfulness
makes us walk together
to meet the challenges on life's journey.
My Divine Faithfulness
will draw you to Me.
for we cannot work in isolation
from each other.
My Divine Faithfulness
is not so much an action as an intuition.
My Divine Faithfulness
becomes a natural part of your thinking.

MY RESPONSE

Write in your journal and/or share in your facebook/ blog what the word "Courage" means to you.

Day 112

FRUIT OF THE SPIRIT

JESUS SPEAKS TO ME OF GENTLENESS

The Gentleness that I give
is the fruit of My Holy Spirit.
My Divine Gentleness
is an expression of the heart.
My Divine Gentleness
encompasses your heart,
therefore your life will be gentle.
If anger encompasses your heart,
then your life will be angry.
My Divine Gentleness
encompasses with the gift of mercy.
You will reach out to help those in need.
My Divine Gentleness
has the meekness of a young lamb
but the strength of a lion.
My Divine Gentleness
encompasses all the fruit of My Spirit:
love, joy, peace
patience, kindness, goodness
faithfulness, and self-control.

MY RESPONSE

Write in your journal and/or share in your facebook/ blog what the word "Gentleness" means to you.

Day 113

FRUIT OF THE SPIRIT

JESUS SPEAKS TO ME OF GENTLENESS

My Divine Gentleness
is coupled with humility.
Humility breaks down pride.
My Divine Gentleness
Is the fruit in which the gift of mercy
operates.
You desire to help those in need.
My Divine Gentleness
is not a sign of weakness
but a sign of strength.
My Divine Gentleness
draws the children onto your lap,
hugs those who are crying,
understands those who are hurting.
It is with My Divine Gentleness
that you will bring healing to many,
that you will perform miracles,
that many will come to know Me.
My Divine Gentleness
is not so much an action but an intuition
that is shown by how you love others.

MY RESPONSE

Write in your journal and/or share in your facebook/ blog what the word "Humility" means to you.

Day 114

FRUIT OF THE SPIRIT

JESUS SPEAKS TO ME OF SELF-CONTROL

The Self-Control that I give
is the fruit of My Holy Spirit.
It is My Divine Self-Control
that sets you free from the bondages
that control your life.
My Divine Self-Control
will give you the strength and the desire
to become free.
The fruit of Divine Self-Control
is at the center of My Divine Image.
In My Divine Image
I gave you the ability to choose.
My Divine Self-Control
gives you the wisdom to choose correctly.
My Divine Self-Control
demands discipline,
but it also gives you the strength
to fulfill the discipline.

MY RESPONSE

Write in your journal and/or share in your facebook/ blog what the word "Self-Control" means to you.

Day 115

FRUIT OF THE SPIRIT

JESUS SPEAKS TO ME OF SELF-CONTROL

My Divine Self-Control
disciplines you
to carry out My plan and purpose
for your life.
My Divine Self-Control
releases you from a past
uncontrolled life
so that you can move on
to a controlled life
under My Holy Spirit.
My Divine Self-Control
gives you hope
because you experience victory.
My Divine Self-Control
is a continuous journey
for we are challenged daily
by the enemy.
My Divine Self-Control
gives you a sense of freedom
which only I can give.

MY RESPONSE

Write in your journal and/or share in your facebook/ blog what the word "Freedom" means to you.

MOTIVATIONAL GIFTS

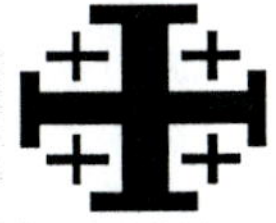

Romans 12:6 - 8 [6]God has given each of us the ability to do certain things well. So if God has given you the ability to **prophesy,** speak out when you have faith that God is speaking through you. [7]If your gift is that of **serving** others, serve them well. If you are a **teacher,** do a good job of teaching. [8]If your gift is to **encourage** others, do it! If you have money, share it **generously.** If God has given you **leadership** ability, take the responsibility seriously. And if you have a gift for showing **kindness** to others, do it gladly.

1 Peter 4: [10]God has given gifts to each of you from his great variety of spiritual gifts. Manage them well so that God's generosity can flow through you.

MOTIVATIONAL SPIRITUAL GIFTS

The Motivational Gifts are the things we do naturally because God has placed them in us by virtue of creation. (Psalm 139) This is the 'DNA' of our lives. These gifts undergird and influence everything we do, the way we behave, think and talk. The Motivational Gifts strongly influence the way we relate to people and how we react to circumstances. Within these gifts we find the area of ministry and career to which we have been called. Our greatest fulfillment is discovering God's plan for our lives and how we can best serve Him. These gifts are for His glory.

1 Corinthians 14: [1]Let love be your highest goal, but also desire the special abilities the Spirit gives.

Check the Internet
Youtube Gifts of the Spirit

Day 116

MOTIVATIONAL GIFT OF PROPHECY

Romans 12: [6]God has given each of us the ability to do certain things well. So if God has given you the ability to prophesy, speak out when you have faith that God is speaking through you.

JESUS SPEAKS OF THE GIFT OF PROPHECY

I have given you the gift of prophecy. This is when I give you thoughts and words so that you may speak My thoughts and words to others which gives glory to My name.

PRAYER FOR THE GIFT OF PROPHECY

Almighty and Eternal God
To some extent You have given all people a measure of the
gift of prophecy.
Lord, no matter how much I have
help me to use this gift to serve others
and to glorify Your Holy Name.
Forgive me, **Father God**, when I misuse this gift
by judging without love,
by accepting the condemnation of others,
by not praising You as often as I should,
by refusing to go to places You want me to go,
by rejecting Your discipline,
by becoming angry and indignant with people,
by becoming discouraged when I see little results.

MY RESPONSE

Write in your journal and/or share in your facebook/ blog what the word "Prophecy" means to you.

Day 117

MOTIVATIONAL GIFT OF PROPHECY

JESUS SPEAKS OF THE GIFT OF PROPHECY

I have given you the gift of prophecy. This is when I give you thoughts and words so that you may speak My thoughts and words to others which gives glory to My name.

PRAYER FOR THE GIFT OF PROPHECY

Help me, **Jesus,** to discover how to use this gift,
by searching Your written Word,
by listening correctly to Your spoken Word,
by being able to discern the spirits,
by being sensitive to Your church, the body of Christ,
by being perceptive to the world around me,
by being sensitive to those You lead to me,
by accepting the authority of Your Word.
Lead me, O **Holy Spirit**
to be bold with the message You give me,
to speak at the right time,
to quickly and accurately identify good and evil,
to hate what is evil,
to encourage repentance that bears fruit,
to grieve deeply over the sins of others,
to be faithful in the prayers of intercession.
This I ask in the name of the Father and of the Son and of the Holy Spirit. Amen

---

MY RESPONSE

Write in your journal and/or share in your facebook/ blog what the word "Bold" means to you.

Day 118

MOTIVATIONAL GIFT OF SERVING

Romans 12: 7If your gift is that of serving others, serve them well.

JESUS SPEAKS OF THE GIFT OF SERVING

I have given you the gift of serving so that you will gladly serve others as you work in My Kingdom.

PRAYER FOR SERVING MINISTRY

Almighty God
To some extent You have given all people a measure of the
gift of serving.
Lord, no matter how much I have
help me to use this gift to serve others and to
glorify Your Holy Name.
Forgive me, **Father God**, when I misuse this gift
by being critical of those who are in leadership,
by judging those whose primary ministry is not
that of serving,
by sacrificing and overlooking the needs of my
family,
by not being willing to give when I know I
should,
by being hurt when others do not thank me,
by not trusting in your power and strength to
provide.

MY RESPONSE

Write in your journal and/or share in your facebook/ blog what the word "Serving" means to you.

Day 119

JESUS SPEAKS OF THE GIFT OF SERVING

I have given you the gift of serving so that you will gladly serve others as you work in My Kingdom.

PRAYER FOR SERVING MINISTRY

Help me, **Jesus**, to discover how to use this gift
by realizing that You came to serve, so I am here
to serve You,
by loving myself so I can serve others,
by accepting service from others with thanks.
Lead me, O **Holy Spirit**
to be perceptive as to who is in need,
to be consistent in prayer to those I serve,
to be loving and willing as I carry out the task of
serving,
to serve only in the strength You give me.
This I ask in the Name of the Father and of the Son and of the Holy Spirit. Amen.

MY RESPONSE

Write in your journal and/or share in your facebook/ blog what the word "Helping" means to you.

Day 120

MOTIVATIONAL GIFT OF TEACHING

Romans 12: [7] If you are a teacher, do a good job of teaching.

JESUS SPEAKS OF THE GIFT OF TEACHING

I have given you the ability to teach others. With this gift I expect you to do the job well and remain true to My word.

PRAYER FOR TEACHING MINISTRY

Almighty God
To some extent You have given all people a measure of the gift of teaching.
Lord, no matter how much I have, help me to use this gift to serve others and glorify Your Holy Name.
Help me, **Father God**, to discover how to use this gift
by following the example of Jesus who is the Great Teacher,
by searching the truth in Your Word,
by being willing to use my gift so others may benefit and grow to maturity,
by living and being an example according to the truth, as I discover it in Your Word,
by sharing in such a way that many may come to know You as Lord and Saviour.

MY RESPONSE
Write in your journal and/or share in your facebook/blog what the word "Teaching" means to you.

Day 121

JESUS SPEAKS OF THE GIFT OF TEACHING

I have given to you the ability to teach others. With this gift I expect you to do the job well and remain true to My word.

PRAYER FOR TEACHING MINISTRY

Forgive me, **Jesus**, when I misuse this gift
by not using the authority of Your Word to
check out my thoughts and ideas,
by being stubborn and therefore not willing to
listen to others,
by being so concerned about material that I close
my mind and do not see the needs of
those I teach,
by using Scripture out of context in order to
prove my point,
by putting myself above others because I feel
they do not grasp things as quickly as
I do,
by being proud and boastful of my capabilities,
by thinking I know it all and being unteachable.

MY RESPONSE

Write in your journal and/or share in your facebook/ blog what the word "Bible" means to you.

Day 122

JESUS SPEAKS OF THE GIFT OF TEACHING

I have given you the ability to teach others. With this gift I expect you to do the job well and remain true to My word.

PRAYER FOR TEACHING MINISTRY

Lead me, O **Holy Spirit**

to use this gift as I teach children and others
who are in need of learning,
to teach with conviction as I follow Your
leading and direction,
to not be ashamed of teaching the truth as
discovered in Your Word,
to teach with genuine love those whom You put
into my care,
to use this gift of teaching only when it is
surrounded by the fruit of the Holy Spirit:
LOVE, JOY, PEACE,
PATIENCE, KINDNESS,
GOODNESS, GENTLENESS,
FAITHFULNESS AND
SELF-CONTROL.
This I ask in the Name of the Father and of the Son and of the Holy Spirit. Amen.

MY RESPONSE

Write in your journal and/or share in your facebook/ blog what the word "Discovery" means to you.

Day 123

MOTIVATIONAL GIFT OF EXHORTATION

Romans 12: [8]If your gift is to encourage others, do it!

JESUS SPEAKS OF EXHORTATION

I have given you the ability to encourage and to pat people on the back. This is necessary so that people can feel good about themselves and not get discouraged.

PRAYER FOR THE GIFT OF EXHORTING

Almighty and Eternal God
To some extent You have given all people a measure of the gift of exhortation.
Lord, no matter how much I have, help me to use this gift to encourage others and to glorify Your Holy Name.
Help me, **Father God**, to discover how to use this gift
by encouraging others daily so that none may be hardened by sin's deceitfulness,
by being positive in my own attitude toward the church and toward life, believing that "with God nothing shall be impossible."
by following the examples of Jesus and other saints like the Apostle Barnabas who constantly encouraged those who needed it.

MY RESPONSE

Write in your journal and/or share in your facebook/ blog what the word "Encourage" means to you.

Day 124

MOTIVATIONAL GIFT OF EXHORTATION

JESUS SPEAKS OF EXHORTATION

I have given you the ability to encourage and to pat people on the back. This is necessary so that people can feel good about themselves and not get discouraged.

PRAYER FOR THE GIFT OF EXHORTING

Forgive me, **Jesus,** when I misuse this gift
by showing lack of empathy toward those I wish to help,
by being critical and judgmental, especially toward those who disagree with me,
by encouraging selfish motives,
by falling into the trap of being over-talkative, which often leads to gossip,
by being too busy to help those I love and those you place before me.

MY RESPONSE

Write in your journal and/or share in your facebook/ blog what the word "Criticism" means to you.

Day 125

MOTIVATIONAL GIFT OF EXHORTATION

JESUS SPEAKS OF ENCOURAGEMENT

I have given you the ability to encourage and to pat people on the back. This is necessary so that people can feel good and not get discouraged.

PRAYER FOR THE GIFT OF EXHORTING

Lead me, O **Holy Spirit**

to spend time in solitude with You for my own spiritual growth and development,

to live as You have taught me to live and thus encourage others into a closer relationship with You,

to care for the people that I encourage and counsel so they can overcome their problems and difficulties with Your help,

to not overextend myself and burn out as I reach out to others,

to accept people as they are and not try to mold them to my liking,

to be devoted to prayer wherein I find encouragement and inspiration.

This I ask in the Name of the Father and of the Son and of the Holy Spirit. Amen

---

MY RESPONSE

Write in your journal and/or share in your facebook/ blog what the word "Burnout" means to you.

Day 126

MOTIVATIONAL GIFT OF GIVING

Romans 12: [8] If you have money, share it generously.

JESUS SPEAKS OF GIVING

I have given you the gift of giving so that you will have the desire to share with others whatever I have given to you and rejoice when you see people benefit.

PRAYER FOR THE GIFT OF GIVING

Almighty God
To some extent You have given all people a measure of the
gift of giving.
Lord, no matter how much I have help me to use this gift
to serve others and to glorify Your Holy Name.
Help me, **Father God,** to discover how to use this gift
by following the example of Jesus and discovering
what true sacrifice is,
by giving in such a way that I give glory to Your
Holy Name,
by learning that I own nothing, but that all things
come from You,
by being willing to tithe as You have instructed
Your people to do.

MY RESPONSE

Write in your journal and/or share in your facebook/ blog what the word "Giving" means to you.

Day 127

MOTIVATIONAL GIFT OF GIVING

JESUS SPEAKS OF GIVING

I have given you the gift of giving so that you will have the desire to share with others whatever I have given to you and rejoice when you see people benefit.

PRAYER FOR THE GIFT OF GIVING

Forgive me, **Jesus**, when I misuse this gift
by being proud and taking the credit for myself when I give,
by measuring my spiritual success by counting my material possessions,
by judging those who do not give as I give,
by using my giving as a means to control and gain power.
by hording what you have given to me and not being willing to share.

MY RESPONSE

Write in your journal and/or share in your facebook/ blog what the word "Pride" means to you.

Day 128

MOTIVATIONAL GIFT OF GIVING

JESUS SPEAKS OF GIVING

I have given you the gift of giving so that you will have the desire to share with others whatever I have given to you and rejoice when you see people benefit.

PRAYER FOR THE GIFT OF GIVING

Lead me, O **Holy Spirit**

to give of my time, talents and treasures only to those places you want me to give.

to be faithful in praying for those whom I have promised to pray,

to use my gift of giving to discover ways to share the Gospel with others,

to be careful how I spend my own money so I can be an example to others,

to always be thankful to God for whatever I have.

This I ask in the Name of the Father and of the Son and of the Holy Spirit. Amen.

MY RESPONSE

Write in your journal and/or share in your facebook/ blog what the word "Generosity" means to you.

Day 129

MOTIVATIONAL GIFT OF ADMINISTRATION

Romans 12: [8] If God has given you leadership ability, take the responsibility seriously.

JESUS SPEAKS OF LEADERSHIP

I give you the gift of leadership to lead and direct people in righteousness and also to be an influence in the world to bring about transformation.

PRAYER FOR THE GIFT OF ADMINISTRATION (LEADERSHIP)

Almighty God
To some extent You have given all people a measure of the gift of administration.
Lord, no matter how much I have, help me to use this gift to serve others and to glorify Your Holy Name.
Help me, **Father God**, to discover how to use this gift
by realizing that this gift is from You,
by accepting this gift and thus becoming Your instrument in the world of administration,
by coming under Your authority so I do not take matters into my own hands,
by accepting the principle that 'prayer changes things.'
by acknowledging that You are the 'Head' of all administration,
by using this gift in the places of influence in the world.

MY RESPONSE

Write in your journal and/or share in your facebook/ blog what the word "Leadership" means to you.

Day 130

MOTIVATIONAL GIFT OF ADMINISTRATION

JESUS SPEAKS OF LEADERSHIP

I give you the gift of leadership to lead and direct people in righteousness and also to be an influence in the world to bring about transformation.

PRAYER FOR THE GIFT OF ADMINISTRATION (LEADERSHIP)

Forgive me, **Jesus,** when I misuse this gift:
by being critical of those without vision
who find it difficult to change,
by becoming calloused in order to protect myself
from criticism,
by becoming inconsiderate and even hurtful
toward others,
by using people to serve my own purpose,
by over extending myself at the expense of
neglecting my family and my
own health,
by taking the credit myself rather than sharing it
with others and giving You the glory.

MY RESPONSE

Write in your journal and/or share in your facebook/ blog what the word "Critical" means to you.

Day 131

MOTIVATIONAL GIFT OF ADMINISTRATION

JESUS SPEAKS OF LEADERSHIP

I give you the gift of leadership to lead and direct people in righteousness and also to be an influence in the world to bring about transformation to know Me.

PRAYER FOR THE GIFT OF ADMINISTRATION (LEADERSHIP)

Lead me, O **Holy Spirit**
to love, respect and be sensitive to those I work with,
to always call upon the guidance of Your Spirit whenever there is a task to be done or decision to be made,
to be open to the dreams and visions You place before me and then be sensitive to how these need to be carried out,
to receive criticism in a loving way so I do not use my gift to attack,
to use the power you have given me through this gift in a wholesome and constructive way so that others will be blessed,
to carry out the job you have given me in a joyful and enthusiastic manner.
This I ask in the Name of the Father and of the Son and of the Holy Spirit. Amen.

MY RESPONSE

Write in your journal and/or share in your facebook/ blog what the word "Dreams" means to you.

Day 132

MOTIVATIONAL GIFT OF MERCY

Romans 12: [8] And if you have a gift for showing kindness to others, do it gladly.

JESUS SPEAKS OF MERCY

I give you the gift of mercy so that you will have a heart of love that reaches out to those who are in need.

PRAYER FOR THE GIFT OF MERCY

Almighty God,
To some extent you have given all people a measure of the gift of mercy.
Lord, no matter how much I have
help me to use this gift to serve others
and to glorify Your holy Name.
Help me, **Father God**, to discover how to use this gift
by helping others with a spirit of joy and cheerfulness,
by always looking for the good in others,
by always praising God when I see others
who have been blessed by You,
by bringing healing to others in Your Name
as I encounter them.

MY RESPONSE

Write in your journal and/or share in your facebook/ blog what the word "Mercy" means to you.

Day 133

MOTIVATIONAL GIFT OF MERCY

JESUS SPEAKS OF MERCY

I give you the gift of mercy so that you will have a heart of love that reaches out to those who are in need.

PRAYER FOR THE GIFT OF MERCY

Forgive me **Jesus**, when I misuse this gift
by being critical and impatient with my fellow
workers in the field of mercy,
by not being willing to sacrifice
when I know I should,
by making a wrong decision
because I have not consulted Your guidance,
by holding grudges or being critical against
those I feel are wrong or less fortunate,
by being easily hurt and blaming myself
for that which is wrong.

MY RESPONSE

Write in your journal and/or share in your facebook/ blog what the word "Sacrifice" means to you.

Day 134

MOTIVATIONAL GIFT OF MERCY

JESUS SPEAKS OF MERCY

I give you the gift of mercy so that you will have a heart of love that reaches out to those who are in need.

PRAYER FOR THE GIFT OF MERCY

Lead me, **O Holy Spirit**:
to be guided by You whenever there is an
act of mercy to be carried out,
to be sensitive and discerning
when people are hurting,
to consistently pray for those I am aware
of who are in need,
to bring joy and happiness to those
I reach out to help,
to stand up for what is right and good
so people will not be hurting,
to bring all the hurts, pain, and suffering I
encounter to Jesus, who is the great Healer.
to do a random act of kindness each day.
This I ask in the Name of the Father and of the
Son and of the Holy Spirit. Amen.

MY RESPONSE

Write in your journal and/or share in your facebook/ blog what the word "Healing" means to you.

THE JERUSALEM CROSS

By Glen S. R. Carlson

FORMATION OF THE JERUSALEM CROSS

It is comprised of the five Greek crosses and four Tau (T) crosses. The four Tau crosses meet together to form one large Greek cross. The four Greek crosses in each quadrant make a total of nine crosses.

HISTORY OF THE JERUSALEM CROSS

The Jerusalem Cross is like a story that unfolds. It has also been called the Crusaders Cross. The five Greek crosses represent the five nations active in the Crusades: Great Britain, France, Germany, Italy and Spain. The Jerusalem Cross was employed as an emblem by the Crusaders. Godfrey de Bouillon, who became the first ruler of Jerusalem after it was captured from the Moslems in 1099, wore the Jerusalem Cross as his symbol. There are evidences of this cross scratched in the rock that date back to that time. **BY WEARING THE CROSS YOU ARE SAYING,**

"Today I Am A Crusader For Christ."

MEANINGS OF THE JERUSALEM CROSS

1. **PRAYER CROSS** - Pray for Jerusalem (Luke 19:41) Nothing stirs the passions of the devout like Jerusalem (City of Peace) (City of David). Throughout the millennia, nations have warred over it, armies have sacked it, and kings have rebuilt it. Even today, Jerusalem remains a quandary of international diplomacy. Clearly, the Biblical record attests to the lure of Jerusalem; the righteous inhabited it, the pious wept over it. It has

been conquered 37 times in its 3000 year history. At the triumphal entry, Jesus "saw the city and wept over it."

Today I Pray For Jerusalem.

2. MISSIONARY CROSS - Matthew 28
Large Cross - Jesus. Four small crosses - four Gospels (Good News). Message of the Gospel goes to the four corners of the Earth: N,S,E,W.
Acts 1:8 - In the power of the Holy Spirit we go to Jerusalem, Judea, Samaria, and the ends of the Earth.

Today I Am A Missionary.

3. LENTEN CROSS - In Lent we are reminded of the love of God through the sufferings of His Son and we see "The five wounds of Christ:" one on his side, two on his hands and two on his feet.

*Today I Am Willing To
Suffer For Christ.*

4. THE FIVE CROSSES SPEAK OF THE FIVE MINISTRY GIFTS. Ephesians 4:12
God has blessed His Church with Apostles, Prophets, Teachers, Pastors and Evangelists to equip the Saints.

Today I Will Serve Christ.

5. THE NINE CROSSES SPEAK OF THE NINE FRUIT OF THE HOLY SPIRIT. Galatians 5:21-22
Love, Joy, Peace,
Patience, Kindness, Goodness,
Faithfulness, Gentleness, Self-Control.

*Today I Will Live By The Fruit
Of The Spirit.*

6. THE NINE CROSSES SPEAK OF THE NINE MANIFESTATION GIFTS OF THE HOLY SPIRIT. I Corinthians 12
Gifts of Revelation: Wisdom, Knowledge, Discernment
Gifts of Power: Healing, Faith, Miracles